BATTERY
BROTHERS

BATTERY
BROTHERS

STEVEN CARMAN

Battery Brothers
Copyright 2014 Steven Carman

Book format: R.C. Lewis
Cover design by Kirk DouPonce, DogEared Design
Editing: Robb Grindstaff

Elephant's Bookshelf Press, LLC
Springfield, NJ 07081
www.elephantsbookshelfpress.com

ISBN-13: 978-1-940180-04-5

This book is for Kristen, Katelyn, Julie, David, and Ernie.

Many thanks to the countless people who contributed to the inspiration and knowledge and other help in creating this book.

All proceeds from the sale of this book benefit the Sunshine Foundation.

Sunshine Foundation, a 501(c)(3) charity, answers the dreams of chronically ill, seriously ill, physically challenged, and abused children, ages three to eighteen, whose families cannot fulfill their requests due to the financial strain that child's illness may cause.

CHAPTER 1

"SWING LIKE YOU MEAN IT, ANDY," MY BROTHER DANIEL encouraged me. "Pretend the ball's someone you hate."

Hate. I choked up on the stickball bat, thinking of our mother: The Bitch. Yeah, I said it. She was the reason the left side of my face was so messed up. She was the reason for a lot of my problems.

My cousin Craig spit on the blacktop and planted his gorilla-sized sneakers on the chalk-drawn pitcher's line. He stood about six-feet-two and was jacked. Me, I was just a regular-sized seventeen-year-old.

I took some tight half-swings. There was just enough chill in the early March air to cloud our breath.

Rubbing down the tennis ball, Craig smiled like the Grinch. "Two down, nobody on, 7-6—good guys."

If Daniel had been pitching in today's two-on-two, brothers-versus-brothers stickball game, our cousins Craig and

Nathan wouldn't be an out away from victory. Chances are they wouldn't have scored any runs. My brother's 88-mile-per-hour heat would have done the job. But Daniel didn't pitch tennis balls. Not anymore. Not after being tagged a phenom and scouted by the pros. The risk of him throwing out his holier-than-holy arm at the age of sixteen was too great.

"Bring it," I muttered. My left eye twitched at the slap of a gust of wind. The pitch, smoking in high and tight, forced me to backpedal.

I grinned. "In the box?"

"Just missed." Craig scooped up the rebounding tennis ball. The pitcher, having the best view of the 32-by-24-inch box sprayed on the brick schoolyard wall, got final say on balls and strikes.

Daniel clapped. "Keep us alive. We need a big hit here." He put up his sweatshirt hood and rested his tall, wiry body against the brick wall.

Craig raked his fingers through his brown crew cut, a hairstyle that made his broad forehead seem even bigger. My bangs hung to my eyebrows, always getting in the way. But I couldn't see myself in a crew cut. Ever.

Nathan, gawky and pimpled, got into fielding position, drumming his hands on his kneecaps. "Come on, come *on*. End the game here."

I wiggled my fingers around the wooden bat handle, trying to stay loose. "Don't pitch wild like that when *I'm* your catcher, Cuz."

"Andy, you gotta make varsity first." Craig bounced the tennis ball to himself in place. Last year, he'd pitched varsity as a junior.

I looked at the asphalt. "Whatever," I said.

Final cuts were tomorrow. A nerve-wracking way to start the week. I made varsity last year. But that was at my old school, with half the number of kids trying out.

Craig fooled me with an off-speed pitch. My weight forward, I swung under the ball and popped it straight up. Craig reeled it in.

Game over. A sucky loss to complement my sucky life. Which had only gotten suckier when Dad, Daniel, and I moved 350 miles downstate to Collingwood, Long Island. We had little choice. Dad got canned. Couldn't find work. Unpaid bills stacked up and the bank foreclosed on our home.

I was struggling big time to adjust to my new surroundings. Especially at school. Upstate, the students knew me. They knew my face, the burn scar. It was a dead topic. Not down here. At Collingwood High, I was on people's radar, the opposite of where I wanted.

Nathan jogged in, his baggy sweatpants flogging in the wind. A smile tugged the corners of his mouth. "About time we took you guys down."

"Luck," I said, bumping my knuckles into his. Nathan reminded me a lot of myself. He too got the shaft in the DNA gene pool.

We packed up our stuff and piled into Craig's car. It reeked of feet. And judging by the rug, it appeared to have been involved in a flood at some point. At least it was a nicer ride than my junker.

Craig jammed the key into the ignition and cranked up the engine. "Where to, boys?"

"Wanna hit up 7-Eleven?" suggested Nathan.

"Let's do it," Daniel said, his long neck arched forward.

Craig blasted a rap song. The bass in the trunk kicked, rattling the mirrors. I stared out the window, the sprawling high school and its well-kept baseball fields fading into the distance against the backdrop of a low sun. We cruised past nice houses fronted by low-cut hedges and tall trees with swaying skeleton branches.

Craig pulled into the 7-Eleven parking lot, a bit heavy on the gas. Just before the curb, he jerked the car to a stop. His idea of fun, I guess.

I stepped out of the car, focused on my breathing. I was not a big fan of public settings.

As if my anxiety levels weren't sky-high already, Joey Owens exited the store as we approached. I cursed my luck. His fuse was short and he didn't like me. Not a good combination. Before tryouts on Friday, he punched a dent into his gym locker because he thought someone stole his glove. Turned out his glove was in his bag the entire time.

"Ladies," Joey said.

"S'up, big guy?" Craig asked.

Joey dished out high fives to Craig, Nathan, and Daniel. Not that I expected one. He was above certain people. Or so he thought.

Joey had about twenty pounds on me. Was more ripped. A lot more. The school's best wrestler, he placed second at the state competition in the 165-pound division. Now that it was baseball season, he was trying his hand at that. Catcher, to be specific. Yep, same as me.

Joey hoisted his bag of groceries. "Eating whatever I want now that I don't have to make weight."

"Just don't turn into a fat ass," Craig said.

Joey laughed. "Your mom told me she likes me chubby. Actually, she said she likes my chubby."

Chuckles. Even from me. "Keep dreaming," Craig said.

"Hey, enjoy *guys'* day out." Joey winked. "Gotta go. Mandy's waiting." He gestured toward his car, a few parking spots over. A hot brunette fiddled with her seatbelt strap in the front seat.

"Got us there, bud," Craig said.

Eyes narrowed to slits, Joey pointed at me. "Walk with me."

I swallowed hard. This couldn't be good. But you didn't turn down guys like him. While Daniel, Nathan, and Craig entered the store, I followed him to his car.

Joey tossed his groceries into the backseat then slammed the door. He jabbed his finger at the meat of my chest. "You telling people I suck at baseball?"

"No."

"Yeah? Craig says otherwise."

Something in my gut twisted. "I, uh, was just comparing us to Robert. He's really good."

"No, *you* suck. Got it? Just *you*."

"I didn't—"

Joey showed me his clenched fist. "Shut your face. You're lucky I'm cool with your family. That won't save you next time. Bank on it."

I opened my mouth, but rode my words down.

He climbed into his car and drove away. I looked up to the fleeting clouds and puked a little in my mouth. *Damn you, Craig.* Guess I had to watch what I said around my own cousin.

As I entered the store, people glanced at me and looked away. My face had that effect.

Two boys, twelvish, taste-tested flavors at the Slurpee machine. Each wore baggy pants at half-mast and a blue and gray Grovetown Wrestling jacket.

Craig walked up behind the kids, practically breathing down their necks. He growled, "Hurry it up, chumps." He could be a jerk sometimes. In fact, more often than not.

The boys twisted around. The larger one raised his eyebrows. "Screw off."

Craig's face flushed. "Whad'ya say to me?"

He stared Craig down and took a swig of Slurpee.

Craig slapped the bottom of his cup, popping the brim into his face.

The boy raked slush from his cheek. "Dick."

Daniel yanked Craig back. "Relax, tough guy."

The smaller kid set his cup next to the Slurpee machine. "Let's bounce," he said. Then he pointed at me and laughed like a seal as he shadowed his pal out the front door.

My heart sank. Stares I was used to, but a stranger hadn't blatantly mocked me like that in years. My day dove even lower into sucky status. Fast.

Nathan elbowed me. "Punks."

I swallowed past a lump in my throat, forced a smile and browsed a rack of potato chips. Emotions bottled up. Same old story.

We paid for our snacks and drinks and left.

Craig approached his car. "Oh, c'mon. Shit!" A fresh goober trickled down his windshield. He looked left, right. No one in sight.

Craig hopped in and slammed the door. The wipers cleared away the spit, but Craig's ticked-off look remained. He gunned it through yellow lights and around corners until he parked his Escape in the driveway behind my early-model Corolla. A tree's shadow danced on my piss-yellow house, the eyesore of the neighborhood. We were renting from Uncle John and Aunt Sue, Craig and Nathan's parents. They bought the dive as a knock-down-and-rebuild investment, but thus far rented it out as-is.

Craig peered in the rearview mirror. "Am I driving you guys tomorrow?"

"Sure, that's cool." Daniel added curve to the brim of his Mets cap. "How many you think Coach'll keep?"

Craig yawned. "Probably seventeen, like last year."

I felt my blood run cold. I expected a twenty-player team, maybe nineteen. But seventeen players . . .

"I'll be getting cut." Nathan scratched at his triangular nose.

"Um, you told us that before cuts on Friday," I said.

Truth was, Nathan was lucky to have made it to final cuts. Lackluster fielding, little pop at the plate. I just couldn't see Coach keeping him on.

Craig reached between the front seats and shook Daniel's knee. "One thing's for sure. This stud isn't getting cut."

Daniel laughed modestly.

Craig flicked my leg with his finger. "And Coach would have to be brain-dead to cut me. Three complete game shutouts last season. That's right, son."

Just one good punch in the face. That was all I wanted to give my idiotic cousin. "Hey, thanks for telling your pal I said he blows at baseball. He looked ready to rip my head off today."

"Don't mention it." Craig leered. Some family loyalty.

Craig dropped us off then screeched away toward his high ranch on the corner of our street.

"An earthquake hit here?" Daniel asked, kicking up a chunk of driveway pavement that lay loosely in the groove of a deep crack.

I snickered and shook my head. Weeds choked the garden that flanked our moldy stoop. "Place should be condemned."

I pushed the squeaky old wooden door open; the smell of stale cigarette smoke tickled my nose. A gift from the previous occupants.

The furnishings were what you'd expect to find at an old geezer's pad. A sectional couch covered in clear plastic. A grandfather clock. Pull-chain lamps that burned green. Uncle John and Aunt Sue rented the house optionally furnished. A good thing, I guess, since Dad had auctioned off a lot of our crap.

Daniel hung up his coat on a rusty hook screwed into a wall beam. He hustled to the bathroom, the only one in the house.

I booted aside an empty cardboard box that blocked the entrance to our drab living room, sat on the edge of the couch, clicked on the TV and switched to ESPN.

A car pulled into the driveway and I peeked through flimsy plastic blinds. Dad stepped out of his beat-up SUV. I was a cutout of him, just five-eight. Where Daniel got his height from was anybody's guess. If not for his big, crooked-anchor nose, an undeniable family trait, I'd have pegged him as adopted.

Dad popped the hatch and filled his arms with groceries, and I met him outside.

"Hey," I said.

Dark circles underscored his eyes. "Hey, Andy."

"I'll get the rest."

He gave me a wary glance.

Without a word, he and I stocked food into the old metal cabinets. That was until Daniel strutted out of the stunk-up bathroom.

"Ever heard of an air freshener?" Dad asked in a not-so-joking manner.

Daniel shrugged, his palms turned skyward. "There wasn't any. What? It's not that bad."

I fake barfed.

"Shut up." He elbowed my arm as he passed.

Dad pointed at the half-open bathroom door. "Close it."

Not one to talk back, Daniel did as told.

Dad flattened the wispy gray hair rising from his head. "You're on your own for dinner. Overtime tonight."

Dad had his sister's husband, Uncle John, to thank for being back at work. Uncle John put in a good word with a buddy at UPS. So now, the former shop supervisor loaded trucks. But Dad being employed was a blessing. Not just for his sake. He wasn't pleasant to be around when he didn't get his workaholic fix. He was still no ball of joy, but better. No doubt.

He poured himself a glass of water and retreated to his bedroom.

Daniel leaned against the counter, ankles crossed. "Wanna get beat in Xbox?" he asked. "Loser cooks dinner."

"You're going down."

In the fifth inning of our video game, Dad pulled open the front door. He tipped the bill of his brown cap. "Make your old man proud tomorrow, huh?"

He walked out before we had a chance to respond.

Dad was the most apathetic person I knew. Except when it came to baseball. That was where all his passion went. He was a regular fanatic. A diehard Mets fan. A student of the game. He used to coach Daniel and me in Little League, and we won a lot. Nothing brought him greater joy than winning. And nobody wanted to be around him when we lost.

"You going to pitch it or what?" Daniel asked, repeatedly pressing his thumb on the controller button.

I pitched. He didn't swing.

"Hey, you think I'll make it tomorrow?" I asked, my belly flat against the scuffed hardwood flooring.

"Sure. You're better than Joey. Coach'll keep three catchers anyway."

He hit my fastball into the gap for a double, driving in one run.

I gulped. "Robert's damn good. A lock to start at catcher. How'm I gonna get in?"

He rolled his shoulders. "Infield, maybe. Coach'll want your speed in the lineup."

It was hard to tell if he was bullshitting me. As far back as my memory stretched, Daniel and I dreamed of working a no-hitter and winning the high school baseball championship together. This was our final shot. Last season I was benchwarmer. Excusable as a junior, but not this year. Not

---

Dad's eyes. Forget that. And if I failed to even make the team, he'd likely disown me.

Daniel won the game in the bottom of the ninth with a bloop single.

My face went hot. "Damn," I yelled. I banged the remote on the floor and walked toward the kitchen.

"Told you," Daniel said. "Make those mashed potatoes extra fluffy, will ya?"

I flung a couch pillow at him. He swatted it down.

"Wait," I said. "Fluffy? Is that what you said? You fag." I knew the dig would set him off.

He wagged his finger. "Oh, you'll pay."

"Come get it. Scared?"

I got into a wrestling stance, arms clenched at right angles. After we exchanged playful taunts, he faked a dive at my legs. As he straightened up, I shot in at his right leg. He sprawled back before I could lock my hold. In no time, he was behind me and I was on the ground, face-to-face with the worn pinewood. A fury rose in me. I forced my hips backwards into Daniel. Keeping my chest low, I brought my knees under my body.

He gripped me in a bear hug. "Surrender. Or else."

My arms wobbled. "Never."

He pushed off and stood up. "Yo, you bleeding?"

I got up and pawed at my stinging face. "Great."

"Sorry, bro," he said. My face was the only part of me he minded hurting.

I walked into our shared bedroom. I stood in front of the framed mirror propped on top of my dresser, the mirror I'd times than I cared to remember. I even spit on it once. the damage. Just a nick on my cheek. The scarred just below my left eye to under my jawbone. with the corner of my mouth. Surgeries had awful.

I must have really pissed off The Bitch for her to take a hot iron to my face. It wasn't like I was even old enough to defend myself. My skin melted. I almost died. Sometimes I wish I had. She served time in jail, but she was out now—God knew where. I hadn't heard from her or her family since I was seven.

Daniel joined me in the room. "You okay?"

"It's nothing." I dabbed at the blood with my sleeve.

He looked guilty as sin. "Cool," he said.

"You're lucky. Was gettin' ready to pull a reversal."

Daniel made a face. "*Right*."

We gave each other low fives—three forward and backward slaps—then a sideways chest bump. Something we came up with a few years back.

Until we moved into this hole, we had our own rooms. Nice, spacious rooms. Now our twin beds were a spit's length away, surrounded by cracked baseboards, a filthy window, and an auburn rug worn down to the cement in spots. It was better than living on the streets, though not by much.

I scooped my black catcher's mitt off the floor, touched it to my nose, and breathed in the leather scent. Perfectly broken in. The same glove I'd used the last five years. The glove I hoped to get more use out of after tomorrow. Final cuts.

CHAPTER 2

A CAR HORN BLARED. CRAIG.

"Let's go, Daniel." I snatched my blue Louisville Slugger bat bag off the kitchen table.

Daniel exited the bathroom, mussing with his short, gel-spiked hair.

"You done, pretty boy?"

He smiled wide, showing teeth. "The ladies like a well-groomed man."

"Like you'd know."

At least he'd had a girlfriend. For me, speaking to a girl, any girl, was a major accomplishment.

He swaggered into the living room and gathered his stuff. Trailing me out the front door, he bobbed his head and whistled. *How could he be so happy on a Monday morning?*

I craned my neck, taking in the clear sky and strong morning sun. A chilly breeze wiggled tree branches. I was counting on an outdoor tryout today, but with my luck, the weather would turn and we'd end up in the gymnasium again.

The tailpipe on Craig's car belched smoke. I dropped my bat bag in the trunk, wondering if I should take my own ride. If I got cut, I wouldn't want to be around these guys. Or anyone else.

As I yanked open the rear door, Craig beeped the horn. In a spasm of panic, I shielded my face with my hand and ducked. Ugh. I wanted to disappear.

Hoping this wasn't the way the rest of my day was going to go, I piled inside the car. Tears welled in Craig's eyes and his body hiccupped in laughter.

"Funny." I sat forward, elbows on knees.

Daniel slugged my arm. "Yo, this was you." He launched himself back into the seat, his face contorted.

"Shut up." I shoved his shoulder.

Craig backed out of the driveway. "Today's the day we separate the men from the boys," he said.

Easy for him to say. It was no secret that Nathan and I were the ones on the chopping block.

Nathan muted the stereo. "How'd Coach Fischer do final cuts last year? Post a list or meet face-to-face?"

Craig reclined into the seat, steering with his left hand. "Posted a list."

"Hopefully again," Nathan said. I nodded in agreement.

The closer we got to the school, the more my bowels felt like they were going to collapse. Back upstate, I'd been seeing a psychologist twice a month. Since moving here, I was still talking to him on the phone. He reminded me to avoid anxiety triggers. Not much chance of that when school was one of mine. And now, with a new school to deal with? Major trigger, major anxiety. If it wasn't the urge to take a crap, it was itchiness, feeling like I wanted to puke, or some other symptom. All of them annoying. Last week, he referred me to some woman down here who was supposed to be good. Maybe, but she must not have been so good at fitting new clients into her schedule. Our first session was still a few weeks off.

Craig turned into the school lot and parked in the back row, the spaces unofficially reserved for the cool kids' cars.

I climbed out, phantom hands clenching and flipping my guts.

Tommy Goodwin, last year's starting third baseman, roared his Mustang into the spot next to me. Tommy was a chubby kid with a round face and thick sideburns. The team goofball. When he got hold of the ball, it rocketed off his bat. Unfortunately, he whiffed often and ran at a snail's pace.

Tommy emerged from the car. "What up, ladies?"

Craig sneered and gave him the finger.

I lifted my bat bag out of the trunk. "Gotta hit the bathroom. Later, guys."

"Later," Daniel and Nathan echoed.

They stayed and chatted while I marched off, praying I'd make it before my pants turned a darker shade of brown.

My new school was chock full of preppies, just like the entire town of Collingwood. Happy people, happy town. Gag me. I swung open a main entrance door and hustled down the gleaming corridor that reeked of bleach. I could feel their glances on me.

Once inside the bathroom, I made a beeline to an open stall. My butt landed on the bowl just in time. Breathing fast and hard, I rubbed my hands up and down my bare thighs. I kept telling myself to calm down. Sweat beaded on my forehead. My stomach churned. Not a good start to the day. Not at all.

I slouched at my desk in my fourth period math class, the second hand on the wall clock ticking toward the finish line. The bell rang. Lunchtime. Morning classes were blah. I was my usual zombie self, saying nothing, doing my time. At least my stomach felt better. I won the race out the door and cruised down the hallway, weaving around slower traffic.

Nathan spun the dial at his locker. He looked a lot like what I imagined Bill Gates looked like as a teenager. Tousled hair, wrinkled clothes, pimples, the works.

I clapped my hand on the hard bone of his shoulder.

He glanced at me. "What's doing?"

"You headed to lunch?"

"Yep. What's on the menu?"

"Sloppy Joes."

He rolled his eyes. "I'll stick with my brown bag. Thanks."

I nodded. "Probably for the best."

After a pit stop at my locker, I shadowed him to the cafeteria. I secured a spot at the end of the hot lunch line. "See you inside," I said.

Craig and Daniel had lunch next period. If Nathan didn't have lunch at this time, I'd have avoided the whole lunchroom experience. Probably spend my time walking around the schoolyard or something.

A heavyset lunch lady mixed the Sloppy Joe meat in a lazy eight and gave me a quizzical look. "What'll it be, Mack?"

"Burger and fries," I said.

She scooped and plopped. I received the plate and slid my tray along the metal rack, adding an apple juice and a pretzel rod. I paid the cashier.

My chest tightened as I entered the crowded cafeteria and spotted Nathan at a table toward the back of the room. He was sitting with his usual crew, Ralph, Donald, and Mark. Brainiacs. Advanced this and college-level that. My grades would get me to graduation. That was about it.

I sat down and scraped the chair up to the table. Ralph

interrupted his take on the national debt to greet me. He was fifty pounds overweight at least, his face sprinkled with acne. "Hey," I squeaked, my body stiff. It usually took me a few minutes to warm-up, even around guys who weren't so cool themselves.

At a table across from us, a couple of kids pounded their fists on the tabletop and chanted, "Do it, do it . . ."

Hailey Baye stood up from that table, her golden blonde hair flowing over her dainty shoulders. She had a perfect body. I didn't know her personally. Only knew of her. She was a hot topic among the guys in the locker room.

She stepped both of her sneakered feet up onto her chair, balanced herself, and said, "Your attention, everyone. Don't forget to check out the book fair today in the gym. All proceeds benefit breast cancer research."

"You're hot, Hailey!" a melon-headed jock from another table responded. A chorus of laughter followed.

Hailey reddened and hopped off her chair.

Ralph cocked his eyebrow. "I'd like to research Hailey's breasts."

We shared a laugh.

I managed to get to the end of the school day without embarrassing myself and went to the varsity section of the locker room. I shuddered at the smell of body odor and oranges. A couple of players were changing into practice clothes. Most hadn't arrived yet, including Daniel, Craig, and Nathan. School ended a period early for me, a senior perk.

Joey, stripped down to his boxers, stepped onto a tall scale and eyed the dial. His back muscles bulged like they wanted out of his skin.

I sat on the wooden bench in front of my locker and kicked off my sneakers.

Joey hopped off the scale and paraded over to me. "Ready to get cut today?"

I forced a laugh, unsure if he was joking.

He shook his head. Then he started talking to the kid next to me, another wrestler.

I made quick work of changing into my sweats. By the time my brother and cousins arrived, my nerves had worked up to the point that my stomach was spin cycling my lunch.

"Enough stretching," Coach Fischer called out. "C'mon, bring it in."

Butt flat against the outfield grass, I reached my fingers to the tips of my cleats one more time, then I hopped to my feet and jogged in, dogged by Daniel.

"Take a knee," Coach said, poking the knob of a metal bat onto home plate. The old man was buff. A thick neck, Popeye arms, not an ounce of flab.

Craig and a few others lollygagged their way in from the outfield.

Coach gave them a steely look. "Got a nice day for ball." He knocked up the brim of his baseball cap with his knuckles, revealing close-cropped gray hair. "Each of you deserves to play at this level. Hardest part of my job is cuts. Show me you want it more. Leave it all on the field. Let's go. Take a lap 'round the far soccer post, then warm up those cannons. We're losing daylight."

I bolted off, erasing the early lead set by a few. My arms and legs pumped hard. No pacing the quarter-mile run today. I threw a glance over my shoulder just before rounding the soccer goal. Nobody close. I floored it back to the baseball diamond, leaving no doubt.

Coach Fischer sat on a shiny, aluminum bench, gazing down at his clipboard. I wondered if he'd caught any part of my run.

I took a breather by the pitcher's mound, my hands locked on my kneecaps. Once I stopped sucking wind, I strode behind the backstop and picked up my infielder's glove.

Daniel jogged over to me. "Wanna throw?"

"Sure."

He shoved on his glove. "You can do this."

I blew out a breath. "I'll do my best."

We trotted out near third base. I threw the baseball to him. He nonchalantly snatched it out of the air, slapping his glove down against his leg. He slung the ball back to me. It popped into my glove, stinging my palm. The kid had an amazing gift.

As we threw the ball back and forth, the tension eased out of my body. There was something about playing baseball that calmed me, something that pushed my usual worries to the side.

"Let's take fielding practice," Coach Fischer said. "Go out to your main position."

I switched to my catcher's mitt, then joined Joey and Robert by home plate. Joey didn't even look at me. Acted like I was invisible.

Coach gave me a sharp stare, his large hands massaging the barrel of a bat. "Take 'em at second base, Andy."

Shit. "Okay."

Something was up. Had Coach decided who the catchers were? Was he checking to see if I could be a utility player? I'd played second base before, but not much.

I changed gloves again and ran to the infield.

Nathan arched his right eyebrow, looked me up and down. "Why aren't you catching?"

"Coach sent me."

The other guys trying out for second base paid me little mind.

Coach fungoed grounders to the left side of the infield first. Solid hits, no weak grounders. He wasn't messing around.

Folding my mitt into itself, I paced small circles where the outfield grass met the infield dirt.

Nathan fielded his grounders cleanly and made decent throws to the catcher and first baseman.

I told the string bean he did a great job then traded spots with him. After scraping a line in the dirt with my cleat, I got into fielding position.

Coach tossed the ball up and whacked it. I moved to my left, cutting off the ball, but a bad hop sent it right through my legs. Damn!

"Let's go. Take another." He hit a whistling grounder. I moved right. The ball in my sights, I dove and stabbed it with my glove. I wrestled up and fired it to Robert at home plate.

"Way to get dirty," Coach said.

"Yeah, nice one, Andy," Nathan added.

I ate up the next grounder and chucked the ball to first.

I muttered to myself and paced behind the other second basemen, pissed that I'd botched the first one.

After we completed game-situation infield/outfield drills, Coach told the pitchers, catchers, shortstops and first basemen to hold their positions. He instructed the others to line up by first base.

Coach waved me in. "Andy, catcher."

I jogged in, trying to keep my nerves in check for a while longer.

From behind the chain-link backstop, Joey and I silently watched player after player try to steal second base on Craig, the pitcher, and Robert, the catcher. If Coach would only let me do some running, I could show him how easily I could swipe second base.

Robert's throws were on the money. He punched out about half the attempts. Solid as usual.

Joey went next, throwing out just one—Tommy, the

turtle. Joey's throws were erratic. The ball seemed to get stuck in his mitt a lot. I suppressed a smile, taking guilty joy in his underperformance. A pitching change brought Daniel to the hill.

Joey stuck out his hand, as if to give me five. But he yanked his hand away as I went to slap it.

Dick.

Crouched behind home plate, I adjusted my mask and held my mitt out steady. No other catcher's gear on.

Daniel, working out of the stretch, kept the runner close to the bag, snapping a few throws over to first. After a quick nod, he smoked an inside strike. I came up throwing, nailing the runner by a good two feet. I allowed myself a slight smile. Coach had to see that. Already I'd thrown out as many as Joey.

I ended up on par with Robert, which was fine by me.

We moved on to hitting practice. Not much daylight left. It became obvious that Coach was only batting and pitching players on the bubble. Nathan, Joey, others batted. Not me. Not yet.

Finally, he said, "Andy, grab a bat."

I darted in from the outfield, my heart beating wildly. After fastening the straps on my batting gloves, I took a few warm-up swings. Ben, a stocky kid with a mess of black curly hair, stood atop the mound.

I stepped into the batter's box, thinking about how much I love this game. The way the bat felt in my hands. The smells. The jargon. The strategy. The pressure. All of it.

I crowded the left side of the plate, my hands jammed together, right elbow cocked.

Ben hurled an outside pitch that escaped Robert's reach and dinked off the bottom of the backstop. Pitch after pitch missed the strike zone. I kept the bat perched on my shoulder. Man, was this guy ever going to give me one?

"You're up there to hit, Andy. Swing," Coach called out.

Shit. These pitches suck.

Ben threw me an eye-level fastball. I chopped it over to the shortstop. I continued to swing at anything close, racking up a few decent hits. But mostly duds and misses.

Then a pitch came right down Broadway. I put my hips into my swing and drove the ball to left field. It landed on the warning track and ricocheted off the fence. That was more like it.

"That's a wrap, guys," Coach said, his right arm raised, a long muscle flexing in his neck. "Meeting in the locker room in a bit."

A shiver ran through me. Cut time.

CHAPTER 3

ON THE BENCH IN FRONT OF MY GYM LOCKER, I WAITED, curling my toes inside my sneakers. Not changing clothes like others were doing. I feigned interest in months-old text messages on my cell phone. My fingernails bit into my palm. My breathing came in quick gulps. I stood up, somewhat lightheaded. *Please, not a panic attack. Not now.* Humming with tension, I shoved my cell inside my dirt-crusted sweatpants pocket and walked out the door and into the non-varsity section of the locker room.

Striding quickly, I gazed at Coach through his office window. He held a phone up to his ear and shook with laughter. Great. While we were sweating it out, he was chatting it up.

I exited the locker room, hooked a left and marched down the school's main corridor, my senses heightened. Aware of every breath. I stopped in front of a display case complete with gleaming trophies, some three feet tall. A photo hung in the center of the display. The 1998 Division IV Champion baseball team. A younger Coach Fischer sat with his team on the gymnasium bleachers. I inched my face up to the glass, my reflection staring back at me. My scar. I could usually be counted on to find some excuse not to make team picture day.

I took a deep breath, knowing I'd better get back.

Coach, not seeing that I was coming, closed the door to the varsity section.

Damn.

I sped up then put on the brakes. A list taped on Coach's door. The list. Breath sawed in my throat.

To look or not to look?

Look.

I baby-stepped, heart sledgehammering.

Please, please, please …

I sucked my lower lip between my teeth. My eyes scanned the list of handwritten names. There was Craig's name. Daniel. Nathan. Robert. Joey.

Shit.

Read it again.

Shit. You've got to be fucking kidding me. Dad's going to …

Moisture filled my eyes. *Don't cry. Don't.* I would rather die than cry in front of the guys.

Coach's speech echoed through the wall, something about nobody having anything to be ashamed of.

Screw you, Coach. Time to walk home. And out I went, past the school buses, through the schoolyard gate, and down the sidewalk along Route 25.

Air whistled through my lips half-sealed with saliva. I turned down a random side street. Then the tears came. A flood of them poured down my ruined face. Blinking rapidly, I lifted my gaze to a buzzing streetlight.

I flicked down my hat, the brim now in my vision. How

did Nathan make the cut and not me? Nathan! And Joey. *Jeez, I must suck.*

My cell buzzed in my pocket. Daniel. In no mood to talk, I powered it off.

At the crest of the hilly block, a garage light lit up. A man dragged his garbage can down his driveway. I wiped away some snot with my sleeve and crossed to the other side of the street.

Get control, Andy. Fucking baby.

The tears dried up by the time I reached Gilmore Street, which I was pretty sure would take me back home.

Dad kept popping into my thoughts, as much as I tried not to think of him. Maybe he'd tell me how he wasted his time coaching me all those years. That I was a complete failure. He'd just be telling me the truth. My grades blew. I was a social retard. A nervous Nelly. Ugly as sin. No friends. No girlfriend. A total mess destined to end up a lonely loser, just like Dad. It was no wonder my mother did what she did to me. I was sure I was a disappointing toddler, too.

Or maybe Dad wouldn't react at all. That'd be even worse. Proof he was immune to my failings and could give two craps at this point. Daniel was his prize. His retirement plan.

I kicked a rock along the curb into a sewer drain. The house to my left looked eerily similar to my old house, from its sloped design to its rustic color. In the driveway stood a minivan with a "Proud Parents" bumper sticker. Behind a huge arching window, a family of five feasted on a meal. All smiles. I coughed hard and wanted to puke.

Bright headlights flashed across my back. I spun around. Craig.

"What's up, cheeseball?" Craig said, driving next to me, his window down.

I stared at my footfalls.

"Done crying it out?" he asked. "Let's go. We wasted enough time looking for you."

I stopped in my tracks. "Leave me alone, 'kay?"

He hit the brakes, poked his head out the window. "Quit being a pussy and get in."

"What?" My throat constricted, I squeezed my hands into tight fists. "Call me a pussy again. Dare you."

He laughed. "Chill, Rocky. I'm just bustin' on you."

Daniel got out and thumped his hand on the car's roof. "Yo, I'll catch up with you guys tomorrow. We'll hike back."

"Your call. Peace." Craig's tires screeched.

Daniel handed me my bat bag. "Forget something?"

"Thanks," I said, head down. "Go ahead. Rub it in."

"You got hosed."

"Ya think?" I rolled my eyes. "Shit, Nathan made it."

Daniel's features closed down. "Problem is Joey's buddy-buddy with Coach. No way he's gonna cut his top wrestler."

"So it doesn't matter that I could steal a base off him while carrying a piano on my back?"

"Apparently not."

I slammed the bat bag down. "It's bullshit. Dad's going to flip."

"Will not. He knows you're a good player."

I ripped my hat off my head. "You don't get it. Baseball's over for me. As of today. The only fucking thing I care about. Gone."

A car drove past us.

"Sorry, bro." He looked like he meant it.

"You'll probably be playing till you're forty. And make a boatload doing it."

He smirked. "Probably."

"Dick." I cracked a smile.

"You know the way home from here, genius?"

I cut my gaze to the street sign. "Gilmore runs into Hammel. I hope."

"Me too."

And Gilmore did run into Hammel. Dad's SUV stood in our driveway. My breaths went shallow.

"Want me to break the news?" Daniel asked.

"Nah."

He followed me in.

Dad sat in his recliner, his feet up, ESPN on the tube. "How'd it go?"

"Great for Daniel." I prodded Daniel's arm.

"And you?"

"Didn't make it."

He jerked the recliner's lever and bounced upright. He looked over his shoulder at me. "What?"

"I didn't make it," I said, louder, on the verge of tears.

"Jeez, Andy."

Nice. "Jeez what?"

"What the hell happened?"

"He got screwed," Daniel said. "Played way better than a catcher with an in with the coach."

Dad coughed, hacked up some phlegm. Swallowed hard. "Stop making excuses for your brother. Andy, you need to get your act together."

"What's that mean?" Anger rose in my chest, choking me.

Dad shifted around in his chair, squaring his shoulders to me. "Look at Daniel. Straight A's. Recruited by Ivy League schools. The Majors. He's going places. And you? Have you even started applying to colleges?"

I felt his words in my back. "Ain't going."

He turned away from me, his attention revived by the TV. "No college, and your free ride ends. Come next year, you'll pay to live here."

"Don't worry. I'll be outta here by then. For good."

He cranked the volume to an ear-piercing level.

Fighting the urge to punch my hand through the wall, I stormed off to my bedroom. Slammed the door. Gave my dresser a kick. I knuckled moisture from my right eye. I hated my fucking life. Hated it!

I leaned against the dresser and listened to Daniel ask Dad to lower the volume. Then Daniel shouted, "What's wrong with you?"

The TV went mute. I didn't move.

"Mind repeating that?" Dad said.

"Andy just got cut. You had to start with him?"

I couldn't believe my ears. Daniel talking back to Dad, sticking up for me?

"Your brother needs people to stop feeling sorry for him. To stop blaming others. I'm tired of the pity party."

"He played his heart out."

The TV volume went back up. I sat down on my bed. Daniel opened the door, walked in, and gave the door a slam of his own.

"Thanks, man," I said.

He arched his eyebrows. "You want me to get you on?"

"Huh?"

"On the team."

"What?" I asked, scrunching my nose.

"I'll tell Coach we come as a package. No you, no me."

"Are you high?"

"Shut up. Want me to do it?"

Who was this guy and what did he do with my spineless brother?

"I'm not a charity case, but thanks. I'll get a job, save till I can get the hell out of here."

"You sure?"

"Never more."

He pursed his lips and nodded hard.

I grabbed my laptop off the nightstand and made myself comfortable on the bed. Thankfully, Aunt Sue and Uncle John rent this dump Wi-Fi enabled.

I went online and chatted with Nathan for a few minutes. Mostly about me not making the team. And about him making it. I wrote what he wanted to read. That he deserved it. That I was fine. That I didn't care. I typed, I lied.

CHAPTER 4

I
N THE LOBBY OF AN OFFICE BUILDING, I SAT ON A WIDE
armchair and grabbed an issue of *Sports Illustrated* from a
stack of magazines on the coffee table.

Directly across from me, the bathroom door swung open.
Joey, of all people, stepped out in his baseball uniform.

I raised the magazine in front of my face and got an all-
too-close look at a photo of Derek Jeter mid-swing. *Please don't
let him see me here. Please.*

"Andy Lembo."

Shit.

"What the heck are you doing here?" Joey asked, striding
toward me, spinning his hat backwards.

I looked at Dr. Steward's closed door, where a sign hung
from the knob: DO NOT DISTURB. SESSION IN PROGRESS.
A white-noise machine sat on the floor next to it, muffling the
conversation on the other side.

Joey smirked. "Should've figured."

"You seeing someone here, too?" I asked hopefully.

He laughed. "No, freakshow. I'm not nuts. My dad's office is down the hall. Just had to pick something up."

My insides burned. "I'm not nuts."

"Sure. I have a baseball game to go play. Enjoy your therapy."

Flushed with rage, I slapped the magazine down and clenched my fists. A part of me wanted to call him out. Right here. To stand up to him. To at least get one good punch in. But what would be the use? Joey would beat me uglier than I already was.

As he walked out, the door to Dr. Steward's office opened. A heavyset, middle-aged man came out. He paid me no mind while he lumbered past and tugged his coat off a metal hanger.

A silver-haired woman appeared in the doorway, bifocals low on her thin nose. "Andy?"

"That's me." I rose to my feet.

"Please, come in."

I entered the dimly lit room, my thumbs circling the pads of my index fingers. Her office was done in shades of brown and the blinds were drawn almost closed, a stark contrast to my former shrink's bright white office.

"Nice to meet you, Andy. Please, make yourself comfortable."

I couldn't explain why, but something about her voice, maybe her calm tone, leached the tension from my face.

I sank into her smooth leather couch.

"Just come from school?"

"Yep. I go to Collingwood."

"A quick drive for you."

"Yeah."

She sat in a swivel chair, five or so feet from me. "I apologize for the delay in scheduling you. Had to put off my current clients, too. But I should be back to a fairly regular schedule now."

"No problem, Dr. Steward."

"Please, call me Mary."

I nodded and chewed on my lips.

"So, what brings you in?" she said, her eyes beaming over her lenses.

I swallowed hard. "I was going to a psychologist upstate before I moved here a few months ago." I dropped my gaze to the brown carpet. "I have some bad days. A lot, actually."

"Depression?"

"Not really. More anxiety. The physical kind. Disruptive. Aches and pains. Nausea. Coughs. You name it."

"Panic attacks?"

"Not often. But yes. They're pure hell. Certain places or things seem to trigger them. Like hospitals."

"Are you on medication?"

"Not anymore. I don't really like being on meds."

"I can understand that." She folded blue-veined hands on her lap. "How have you been adjusting to your new school? A big change, for sure."

"Okay, I guess. Making new friends has been a challenge. Not that I had many upstate."

"And your anxiety?"

"Manageable, I guess."

"What do you do to manage it?"

I shrugged and lowered my hands to the cold leather couch. Damn, I was going to leave sweat marks.

"Luckily, dear, there are endless things you can try. For example, making your diet healthier."

"My diet's horrible. The greasier, the better."

"See? Room for improvement. Do you exercise regularly?"

"I keep in shape, running or whatnot. A lot less now.

Basically, I've been a hermit since I got cut from the varsity baseball team. A few weeks ago."

"Oh, you're a ballplayer."

"I wish. My younger brother's the player. He made the team. In fact, I'll see him pitch his first game after we finish up here. Anyway, he's been scouted by the pros since he turned fifteen. He'll be famous someday. Me, I'm just a sad excuse for a son."

"Why do you say that?"

I turned my head so she could see my full profile. "My mother mistook my face for a shirt. Honest mistake."

She shifted positions, her right leg now crossing her left. "She abuses you?"

"Abused. Not anymore. Haven't heard from her in years. I was freaking two when she did this. Two. Now I'm stuck with this ugly mug."

"I don't see ugliness. A handsome young man, that's what I see."

"Maybe you need a stronger prescription for those glasses."

She tried to suppress a chuckle, but failed. I cracked a smile, too.

Her eyebrows drew together. "What about your dad? Any abuse?"

"No. Sometimes he yells, but he's eased off lately. He's just counting the days 'til I'm not his problem anymore. I'm a senior, so after I graduate, I'll be moving out. No doubt."

"And your plans post-graduation?"

"I can tell you what my plans aren't. School. Getting a job that has anything to do with dealing with the public. I do both now, and I hate it. Maybe I'll have to join the Army. If they'll station me far enough away."

"My oldest son served. Says it was the most challenging, rewarding time of his life."

The more we talked, the more comfortable I felt with Dr. Steward. She didn't judge me. She seemed to really care. We talked about my past some, but mostly about how I could improve my life going forward. I agreed to keep a log of what was going on when my anxiety spiked.

We took care of some insurance paperwork, and we shook hands.

"Have fun at the game, Andy. See you in two weeks."

I pressed the Corolla's gas pedal to the floor as I exited the parking lot, making a left and crossing two lanes of traffic. This fifteen-year-old car had its issues. No oomph. Shook like a druggie when it cruised over fifty miles per hour. It needed a brake job, new tires, and a slew of other things, but I was broke.

I squealed to a stop at a red light. The dashboard clock flashed 3:47. *C'mon light, change.*

I zoomed into a space in the school parking lot, close to a gate leading to the ball fields. I was happy to find the game hadn't started yet.

Debris swirled in the parking lot as I climbed out of the car. Bloated, gray clouds traveled fast. Not ideal pitching conditions for Daniel. Especially since the wind was blowing out for hitters.

I pulled up my hood and followed a sloped, pebbled path that led to the ball field. I looked at my feet while I passed the crowd on the bleachers. I didn't need to see them to sense their stares.

A massive oak tree about twenty yards behind the backstop made for an out of the way spot to watch the game. I checked my phone. No messages.

I spotted Dad over by the bleachers. A closed umbrella hung from his hand. He spotted me. As he made his way toward me, dry leaves clattered under his sneakers.

"Hey," he said, his lips barely parted.

"Hey." If only Aunt Sue and Uncle John could have made it tonight. No such luck.

"Windy." Dad inched down the brim of his faded Mets cap. Brilliant. "Yeah."

"See the scout over there?" His voice had returned to life. Near the backstop, a balding man tinkered with a radar gun.

"Cool," I said. "Team they're playing won the division last year."

"They haven't met the likes of Danny Boy," Dad said, his cheeks pushing up to his eyes. "Let's move closer and see what the scout's clocking him at."

Ugh, spare me.

The hometown Collingwood Panthers, dressed in black and white, took the field.

The Patriots huddled in front of their bench. They piled hands and yelled, "One, two, three, Ward Melville!"

Daniel swaggered out to the mound, his glove tucked under his left arm. Craig, playing right field, exchanged high pops with Jerome Baker, the center fielder. Nathan kept the bench warm with seven other guys.

Daniel hurled some junk pitches to get loose.

"Coming down," Robert called out, straightening his catcher's mask.

Daniel's final warm-up pitch popped into Robert's mitt. Robert sailed a throw the second baseman had to jump to catch.

"This kid made it? C'mon." Dad made a long face long and gestured toward Robert.

I folded my arms. "He's good. Best high school catcher I've seen."

The ump brushed home plate clean. "Batter up!"

A scrawny kid stepped into the batter's box, tapping the tip of his metal bat to the far corner of the plate.

Daniel looked over at me.

I nodded.

41

Dad rubbed his hands together. "This is going to be something."

Daniel wound up, snarled, and smoked a fastball down the middle of the plate. The batter didn't move a muscle. Heck, I don't even think he saw it.

Dad stuck two fingers in his mouth, whistled.

I rolled my eyes.

The batter swung a day late at the next one, the scout's radar gun registering 87 miles per hour. *Sweet!*

A nasty curveball sealed the deal. Back to the bench the batter went, his head down.

The next hitter got a piece of a pitch, fouling it into the backstop. He ended up whiffing, too.

The third hitter, Hobson, looked capable of doing serious damage. Built like an ox, he scraped his cleats through batter's box dirt.

Daniel started Hobson off with a changeup, but he wasn't fooled. He kept his weight back and belted a towering fly ball to left field. Pete raced to the wall. The ball landed safely in his glove. Disaster averted.

Hobson took the mound for Ward Melville, his jaws working a wad of gum.

The scout clocked Hobson's pitches to the first two batters before putting the radar gun away. Hobson's fastballs averaged mid-seventies, fine for high school baseball, but not quite professional grade.

The Panthers and Patriots exchanged goose eggs until the bottom of the fifth. That was when Craig ripped a double into the left-center-field gap, driving in two runs. Cheers echoed, but Dad's hooting after the crowd noise died down soured my short-lived joy.

Craig stood on second base, bobbing his head like the cocky bastard he was. Jerome kept the two-out rally going with a single up the middle, driving in Craig. Daniel ended the inning, taking a called strike three.

The score remained 3–0 going into the top of the seventh inning, Ward Melville's last chance. Dark clouds had piled up. The breeze carried the smell of rain.

Daniel worked quickly. Two pitches. Two groundouts.

The crowd stood, anticipating their hometown Panthers taking down last season's division champs in the opener. But Daniel disappointed them, walking the next two batters. He was showing signs of wear, his velocity dipping into the low-eighties. And Hobson, one of two Patriots with a hit off Daniel, stood on deck. Robert flipped up his mask and jogged out to the mound.

Damn, I should have been the one out there reassuring him.

After a brief chat, Robert walked back behind the plate, fiddling with his chest protector.

Daniel pushed out a breath then hurled a pitch that Robert had to stand up to catch.

Hobson stepped out of the batter's box, grinning.

Shit. "Come on, Daniel," I called out, my shyness taking a backseat to my brother's pitching woes. Fan this chump. Daniel, a strikeout shy of a dozen for the game, hadn't gotten Hobson to swing and miss yet.

Daniel locked his eyes on his target. *Go with the heat. No games, bro.*

He threw a curveball. Hobson kept his weight back and punched a whistling line drive to left field. It one-hopped into Pete's glove.

I felt my heart accelerate.

Pete chucked the ball to Mike Kane, the cutoff man.

The speedy lead base runner blew through a stop sign from the third base coach.

Kane relayed it home to Robert on a rope.

Steps before home plate, the runner stumbled. He tumbled

awkwardly into Robert, then onto the plate. Robert went down and the ball popped out of his mitt.

The ump signaled safe.

Daniel picked up the ball, guarded home plate then called for a time out.

Coach Fischer ran out, arms flailing, yelling to the ump that the runner had barreled over the catcher and should have been out. But Coach's attention quickly switched to his catcher. Robert was still down.

Our team's trainer hustled out to check on Robert. A few moments later, Robert stood, his arms hooked around the shoulders of two teammates. With help, he limped to the bench.

Joey frantically worked to slap on catcher's equipment.

Just my luck. If I'd made the cut, I'd have been in there.

Fully padded, Joey raced out to the mound for a chat with Daniel.

"One more out to go, Danny," Dad called out.

I shook my head. I hated to see him so interested.

Working out of the stretch, Daniel eyed the runner taking a conservative lead off third base. He threw a pitch outside of the strike zone, but the hitter chased it, tapping a slow roller back to the mound. Daniel fielded it, flipped to first. Game over.

After slapping hands with the opposing team, Daniel jogged over to the bench and gabbed with Robert. Robert pulled down his sock, revealing a bulge on his hairy ankle.

Then the bottom fell out of the sky. Heavy rain blowing sideways made my sweatshirt stick to my chest like a second skin.

Dad snapped open his umbrella. "Gotta plan, Andy."

"Right," I said and darted off. Passing the bench, I yelled, "Nice game, bro. I'm outta here."

Daniel gave me a thumbs-up, a puddle of mud forming at his feet.

In sixth-period gym class, my sneakers squeaked on the glossy hardwood floor. The point guard passed me the basketball. At the top of the key, I turned and heaved a jump shot that clanged off the front of the rim. Charging in for the rebound, I tripped over the extended leg of Raymond, who had been on my case all game, and hit the deck. I guessed he was still sour over me rejecting his first shot right back into his fat face.

I pushed myself up off the floor and gave him a cut-the-shit look. He stepped into my path. "Whatchya looking at?"

I glared. "Not much."

"Wait. Now I know who you remind me of. That elephant guy."

My confidence soared on a sports-induced adrenaline high. Snarling, I drove my palm into his sweat-soaked shoulder. Hard. "Say it again, your teeth go down your throat. Got it?"

Raymond said nothing, his eyes large with shock and fear.

I maintained a serious look, hoping Raymond was the coward I figured him to be.

Coach Fischer blew his whistle twice, halting play throughout the gymnasium. But Coach wasn't focused on the others. He was focused on me. "What's the problem?"

"No problem."

He checked his watch. "That's time for today. Balls back on the rack. Volleyball next Friday."

Raymond's lips formed a twitchy smile. "It was a joke. No need to get your nuts in a knot."

I untucked my shirt. "Whatever. Nice game."

On my way off the court, Coach called my name.

I looked over my shoulder. "Yeah."

"My office. After you get changed."

Screw off, old man. "'Kay."

After changing into my school clothes, I stood in front of Coach's closed door. I took a deep breath and knocked lightly, two taps with a knuckle.

"It's open."

I tried to make my expression wooden, and entered.

"Take a seat."

I sat on a plastic chair.

He leaned forward in his chair, his thick forearms resting on the edge of the metal desk. "Any idea why you're here?"

Um, because you told me to come. "Yeah. Well, Raymond purposely tripped me."

He chuckled. "Not that. How about joining the baseball team?"

Ice shot down my spine. "Huh?"

"Robert's done for the season. Fractured ankle."

I slid my hand up my forehead, hiking up my bangs. "Did Daniel tell you to do this?"

More laughter. "I call the shots."

"But he asked."

"He did. We have a talented squad, but a little thin at catcher now."

"Daniel threatened not to play. Right?"

Eyes tight, he said, "No. You're a good player. I want you on the team."

My body tingled with excitement. "Really? You want me to play on varsity?"

"Yes, son. Soon as today. We're home versus Kings Park."

My heart leaped into my throat. "Today?"

"Interested?"

Holy shit. A part of me wanted to tell him to shove it, to deal with the team he'd chosen. But not a very big part. For better or worse, baseball was in my blood.

I nodded. "Sure, I'll play."

"Good man. I assumed Robert at catcher every game. Not much a fan of keeping kids on the bench all year. Especially seniors."

I nodded some more.

"Now it's open competition. Joey'll get first shot, but I'll keep an eye on you in practice."

Nice. "I'll do my best."

He winked. "Let's get you a uniform, eh?"

I wiggled my house key into the knob and elbowed open the front door. Bright sunlight sliced into the foyer.

Breathing deep, I walked in and placed my gym bag on the kitchen table. Bile shot up into my mouth. I swallowed it back down. Acid burned my throat. The toilet beckoned. I ran to it. Don't. Don't vomit, pussy. Get control.

I couldn't play ball like this, my stomach churning, choking down lunch. Puke roared out like water from a hydrant. I coughed, spit, and flushed.

There were times in my early teens when I had puked twice a day for weeks on end. Doctors ran all kinds of tests on my digestive system. They all came back normal. Which made sense now, knowing the real problem was in my head.

I cleaned the toilet bowl so Dad and Daniel wouldn't notice later.

At the bathroom sink, I splashed cold water on my face and looked in the mirror. The reflection didn't lie. I was looking at a freak.

I dried off and killed the light. I closed the bathroom door behind me and leaned back against it. I squeezed my eyes shut and spun my thoughts, the way my doctors had trained me. I needed to take slow, deep breaths. Get dressed. Get pumped for the game. Go out and play the game I loved more than life.

CHAPTER 5

I
N THE SCHOOL PARKING LOT, I SAT ON MY CAR'S REAR BUMPER
and slipped my feet out of sneakers and into cleats. Down
the hill, a handful of my teammates filed out of the locker
room as others loosened up on the diamond.

Uncle John drove his black Hummer through open gates.
Aunt Sue, riding shotgun, snapped down the sun visor. They'd
left work early to make it in time for Craig's first pitch.

I zipped up my bat bag.

Uncle John pulled up beside me. A burly man, he scratched
at his thick red stubble.

Aunt Sue, nearest me, lowered her window and squinted.
The sun highlighted splashes of gray in her curly brown hair.
"Andy, is that you?"

I stood up, smiling. "No, it's the other kid with an ironed
face."

She laughed, dangling her bracelet-laden arm out the window. "What's going on? Why the uniform?"

I looked down at my jersey, the word "Panthers" scripted across the chest. "I'm on the team. As of today."

"Get out. That's fantastic. Did you hear that, John?"

Uncle John leaned toward me. "Yeah. Good luck, kid. Your old man coming?"

"After work."

"Great," Aunt Sue said. "We'll see you down there, sweetie."

"'Kay. Later."

A school bus turned into the parking lot. The Kings Park Kingsmen.

My bat bag tugging hard on one shoulder, I headed down to the field. Bats pinged and gloves popped. My heart did its best to burst through my chest.

I stepped over the chalked baseline. My cleat dug into fair-territory grass. A shiver slid down my spine.

Daniel stood in the outfield, stretching his hamstring. He glanced at me, then away. Then the double-take.

I tipped the bill of my hat.

Jogging toward me, Daniel flashed a smile so bright I could feel its glow.

I kept my face serious.

"Dude, what are you doing here?"

"What does it look like? Didn't think I was going to let my little bro win a championship alone, did ya?"

He lowered his hand to the ground and we did our special handshake, topped with a chest bump.

"Holy crap. Why didn't you tell me? Did you tell Dad?"

"Nope."

"What number you got?"

I spun around.

"Five. Sweet."

"David Wright, baby."

Craig swaggered over. "Yo, Andy. JV is *across* the street."

I chuckled.

"Welcome aboard," Pete hollered from the outfield.

I raised my hand in acknowledgment.

Craig extended his hand. "Put 'er here."

I gave him five.

"So what's this? You on the team?"

"Nothing gets past you." I bumped my forearm into his unyielding shoulder.

"Got Daniel to pull some strings for you, huh?"

I cut my gaze to Daniel.

"Stop. I didn't."

Something about the way he said it didn't ring true.

"Right," Craig said, sidestepping, skipping away from me. "Just make sure you keep that bench warm for me." He fled to the outfield.

I hardened my look at Daniel.

"Honest."

"You know, if you blackmailed Coach to get me here, I'll break that million-dollar arm of yours. I will."

He stuck out his fist. "I know."

I knocked his knuckles. "Wanna throw?"

"Yeah, let's throw."

After meeting with the ump, Coach called us in. We gathered behind the backstop.

"Take a knee," Coach said.

We all got down.

"First thing." Coach's lips were a straight line. "We have a new addition. Andy, welcome."

I nodded, my face going hot.

Heads turned toward me. Nathan nudged my arm.

"Kings Park's throwing Gardner. He's got decent stuff, but can get wild. Take a strike till I say otherwise."

Coach rattled off the starting lineup, top to bottom. Pete Pixcell, leftfield. Mike Kane, shortstop. Jake Murphy, first base. Tommy Goodwin, third base. Craig Huckabee, pitcher. Jerome Baker, centerfield. Kevin Cross, second base. Joey Owens, catcher. Paul Winsor, right field.

Huh? No Daniel? Granted, Daniel's hitting was mediocre at best. And he's been known to botch the occasional fly ball. But he's a better choice in right field than Paul Winsor. No doubt.

Coach's speech droned on. He spoke of the ground rules and such and concluded with a hearty, "Let's go. Play hard."

We pushed into a circle, hands piled in the middle. Craig led the cheer. "One, two, three, Panthers!" In sync, we heaved up our arms. The starters took the field.

Nathan dropped his hand on my shoulder. "Great to have you on, Cuz."

"Why's that? Company on the bench?"

He smiled. "Heck yeah."

Aunt Sue waved from the bleachers.

Daniel perched on our team's bench and picked up a filthy, shredded baseball.

I sat next to him. "You kidding me? He's not playing you in right field?"

Eyes pinched, skin wrinkled at the corners, Daniel said, "Obviously."

I lowered my voice. "Jeez, this guy's clueless."

He elbowed me, his face drawn. "Easy. You just got on.

Saying stuff like that'll guarantee that uniform of yours never gets dirty."

"Puh-*leeze*."

Nathan plopped down next to me. "Told you, Andy. A great view."

"Yeah." I looked over my shoulder at the crowd filling the bleachers. An attendance of zero would be ideal.

"Wanna do the honors?" Nathan asked, poking me with a corner of the scorebook.

"Nah."

"You keep the book," Daniel said, looking sideways at Nathan. "Good grief, I've seen Andy do math. We don't need the other team getting bonus runs."

Joey, clad in catcher's gear, grabbed his glove off the bench and shot me an evil look.

That's right. I'm here, ready to take your starting position. Enjoy your time on the field while it lasts, asshole.

I wondered if he told others I was in therapy as he made his way out to the field. If the whole team knew. I'd bet on it.

Daniel stood and reached into his back pocket. He shook out a ratty, child-sized batting glove.

"Still got it?" I asked.

"You know it. Hasn't failed me yet."

The batting glove was too small to fit Daniel's hand anymore. But that didn't matter. It was magical, capable of taking Daniel all the way to the pros. Help him rewrite the record books. Or so Grandpa Bill, the man we called Big B, claimed when he gave Daniel the batting glove on Daniel's eighth birthday. A month later, the Big C claimed Grandpa Bill's life. In memory of him, Daniel religiously parked the batting glove in his rear pocket on game days. And heck, maybe it really worked.

By the time Craig finished his warm-up pitches, the rest of the non-starting Eagles claimed a spot on the bench. A solid bunch, worthy of starting on most other varsity baseball teams. But not on this stacked team.

Craig stomped his left cleat clean. Gazing out at the crowd, he nodded hard, eating up the attention.

"Showboat," I said.

Nathan made a face. "Craig? Nah, never."

We shared a laugh.

I poked Daniel's arm. "Is there practice tomorrow?"

"Nope. Coach is away this weekend."

I pushed out a breath. "You still wanna practice tomorrow? Maybe Coach'll let us use the batting machine."

Daniel leaned forward. "Sure. *You* ask him."

Kings Park's leadoff batter settled into the batter's box. Short and slender, he wiped his chin on his collar.

Craig rocked into motion, fired a called strike. The crowd hooted and echoed Craig's name.

The batter ended up grounding out weakly to the first baseman. A pop out to left and a tapper back to the mound made for an easy first inning.

Strutting off the field, Craig lifted his cap, saluted the crowd. A big, goofy smile.

Gardner took the mound for the Kingsmen. Tall as Daniel, Gardner packed extra pounds. Mostly in the gut.

Pete, a speedy peanut of a guy, jumped on Gardner's first pitch, dumping a base hit to left field.

Pacing the third base coach's box, Coach looked ready to storm across the field and strangle Pete.

"Here," Coach said, nostrils flaring, beckoning Mike Kane.

Mike ran out to Coach, the barrel of the bat cupped in his right hand.

Coach talked and Mike listened. I was pretty sure Mike was advised to take a strike or else.

Mike wisely let the first pitch go by, an eye-level fastball.

Three more wild pitches followed. The walk parade started. Gardner was all over the place, even beaned Jerome. We ended up plating five in our half of the first.

The pace of the game picked up. Gardner found his groove. Craig never lost it. At the end of five innings, we had a comfortable 8-2 lead.

My butt grew numb on the bench. In the crowd behind me, I didn't see Dad. I couldn't remember the last time he missed one of Daniel's games.

The starting Panthers took the field. Coach strolled in from the coach's box, his eyes scanning the benchwarmers. "Lembo. Get out there."

Lembo. That was me. My breath stuck in my throat.

"Take right," Coach said. "Tell Winsor to come in."

Daniel hopped up. "Later, dudes." He was gone in a flash.

I flicked Nathan's shoulder. "Thought he was talking about me."

Nathan stood and tucked in his jersey. "Your time will come. Trust me."

I nodded. Joey was having a crappy game. Hitless at the plate. Hadn't thrown out any steal attempts.

Coach took a seat next to me on the bench. My body went stiff.

He turned toward me. "I'm looking forward to see what you do at the plate in practice. You're solid enough behind it."

"Okay." Damn, a stupid response.

Coach browsed papers on his clipboard. My gaze swept across the field. Players in motion. Symmetry. Where I should be.

"Coach," I said, trying to buttress my voice.

He looked at me.

"Heard there's no practice this weekend. Any chance Daniel and I could use the batting machine?"

He leaned forward, elbows on knees. "Stop by my office

after the game. I'll give you the key. Make sure the shed gets locked."

"Will do. Thanks."

Coach stood up, his steel eyes on me. He nodded and walked away.

Nathan put the scorebook down on the bench. "That's cool. Wish I could come. Lord knows I could use the practice."

"Your dog's competing in Jersey, right?"

"Yeah, my mom's nuts. But it's kind of cool, seeing Buster leap hurdles and crap."

I smiled. "Sounds it."

In the bottom of the sixth, we broke the game open. Seven Panthers crossed home plate.

Between innings, Coach told Craig to take a seat and sent in a reliever to close out the game.

Craig squeezed himself between Nathan and me on the bench. Sweat flattened the hairs on the back of his neck. "That's how it's done, boys."

"Nice job," I said, wanting to slap the smug look off his face.

Craig leaned right and bumped me. Then he leaned left and bumped Nathan. "Space out. Jeez."

I slid over some.

The first batter laced a single up the middle.

Craig chewed sunflower seeds, spitting the shells. "He better not blow my lead. That's all I'm saying. How many Ks I end up with?"

Nathan calculated. "Four."

"That's it? Damn, Daniel's double mine."

Triple.

Craig gave his parents a wave. "Where's your old man?" he asked. "You tell him you're on the team yet?"

"Not yet."

The middle infielders turned a nifty, highlight-reel double play—Kane to Cross to Murphy. The final out came on a high fly to center field that landed squarely in Jerome's glove. I joined my teammates on the field, feeling more like a cheerleader than a player. We lined up and clapped hands with the Kingsmen.

While packing up gear, I turned to Daniel. "It's weird Dad never showed."

Daniel unhooked the water cooler from the fence, dropped it to the ground. "He called Aunt Sue. Said his clunker clunked out."

"Figured something. Dad misses parent-teacher nights. Not your games."

Daniel dumped the water, muddying the dirt before him. "What, were you worried about him or something?"

I made a sound like air being released from a tire.

Craig walked toward me, pointing. "Newbies take in the bases."

"Yeah, I'll get 'em." Hell, I was eager to do anything to help out the team. My team.

CHAPTER 6

I CLOSED THE FRONT DOOR AND DROPPED MY BAT BAG IN
the foyer.

Dad shifted in his recliner, swung his eyes toward me.
"Halloween's in October, you know."

I chuckled and pulled my jersey straight on my shoulders.
"I'm on the team. Varsity."

"Huh? You played?"

"The bench. But, yeah, I'm on the team. Coach asked me.
Backup catcher for now."

A smile softened his face. "No shit. You win?"

"Creamed them."

"How'd Danny play?"

"Good."

Daniel barged through the front door. He hopped behind
me and shook me by my arms. "You see this kid? The Lembo
brothers are back in full force."

Dad stood, his bloodshot eyes forced wide, and glared at me. "Don't screw up. There won't be a third chance."

I nodded.

Dad rubbed the back of his head. "My car's done. The tranny went. I'll need to use the Corolla for a while."

I rolled my eyes. "Good luck. It's on its last legs, too."

Dad hitched up his belt. "You'll have it back soon enough. After the bat sells."

Daniel and I looked at each other, then back at Dad.

"What do you mean?" Daniel asked.

Dad sat in his recliner, hands turned up on his knees.

I said, "Dad, don't."

Dad spoke over his shoulder. "It's just going on vacation."

"What?" I asked.

He locked his gaze on Daniel. "Till Danny makes the bigs. The mega bucks. You'll find it, buy it back. Won't you, son?"

"Sure. But—"

"But nothing. Conversation's over."

"Dad, you—"

"Maybe you didn't hear me. I said the conversation is over."

And that was that. Dad didn't speak about the bat. Or about his brother Bruce. But we knew. A few years ago, Aunt Sue clued Daniel and me in to story of the bat. It went down in the summer of 1976. Dad and Aunt Sue's brother was nine years old. He was scheduled to undergo his third heart operation, the most risky yet. Dad, thirteen, had a plan. He wrote the Mets' organization daily. Pleaded for them to send something, anything, signed by Tom Seaver. Bruce's idol.

A day before the operation and still no package from the Mets. Dad, fed up, had his dad, my Grandpa Bill, sign a ball in Tom Seaver's name. Later that night, Tom Seaver showed up at their house—dressed in street clothes, holding a bat. A bat signed by the entire 1969 Mets championship team. Aunt

Sue said she had never seen her brothers so overjoyed, smiles so big.

Bruce didn't make it through the operation. And per Aunt Sue, that's when Dad's black cloud arrived. The same cloud that hovered over his head now.

Morning sunlight streamed through the living room blinds. Seated on the plastic-covered couch, I rubbed my eyes. Daniel, standing flatfooted on the hardwood floor, pressed his fingertips to the top of the doorway frame. "Ready?"

I clicked off the TV. "Let's do it."

"Don't forget the shed key."

"Got it." I patted my sweatpants pocket.

Dad chomped Cheerios at the kitchen table.

"You need the car today?" I asked.

Dad shot me a guarded look. "I got somewhere to go at three."

"Can I use it this morning? We wanna get in some BP at the school."

"Thought there was no practice this weekend."

"There isn't. Just shakin' the cobwebs off."

Dad pointed his spoon at me. "Be back by three. Not a second later."

"Will do."

It took two tries for the engine to turn over. Heat blew strong from the vent. Fog cleared from the windshield, center outward. Once my peephole was big enough, I backed the car out of the driveway.

Daniel changed the radio to AM, spun the dial to Sports Radio 660, WFAN.

"I'm gonna work on hitting opposite field," I said.

"Me too. I pull everything."

I checked the gas gauge. Half a tank. "How fast does the pitching machine get up to?"

"Hundred." His eyebrows bounced up and down. "We should crank a few."

I smiled. "I'm game. Hey, think Dad'll really sell the bat?"

Daniel cleared his throat. "Who knows? Hope not."

"He must be in it deep."

As we merged onto Veterans Highway, thoughts of Bruce pecked at my brain. Visions of the open-heart operation.

Heart conditions are hereditary.

In a flash, my body switched to defense mode. I became all too aware of my heartbeats. My face went hot. Tension weighed on my shoulders like sandbags.

Fucking anxiety.

I sank my fingernails into the steering wheel.

Stop. Everything's fine. I'm totally healthy. There's no way something's wrong with me. Impossible. Madness. Think of something else. Ugh, I could have a heart attack while driving, kill people on the road. Kill myself, my brother.

I signaled and shifted to the right lane. I imagined the accident scene. A metal guardrail stuck through my torso and Daniel's neck. Blood everywhere.

Shit.

Sweat dampened my face, clung to my back, my body stiff.

"You okay?" Daniel asked.

"I'm fine," I muttered.

"You don't look fine."

I threw him a glance then looked back at the road.

Lightheaded, I concentrated on the slow flow of my breathing. I opened my mouth and drew in a big breath. Air lodged in my tight throat.

No, God. I'm not taking in enough air. I'm going to freaking pass out.

I steered with my right hand, tapped the side of my neck with my left. Twisted and untwisted my mouth.

"Dude, something's off with you." His voice wavered.

I didn't answer.

I'm fine. I'm freaking fine. I'm in control.

The school loomed in the distance, winking through tall trees. I blew out a long, calming breath.

I'm going to make it.

After I parked, I released my death grip on the wheel and switched off the ignition.

Daniel sat beside me, his spine erect. His droopy eyes swiveled toward me. Silence stretched between us.

I cued my tough-guy voice. "Got a staring problem?"

"We can practice tomorrow."

"Shut up." I pushed the door open, climbed out. With each step, I denounced dizziness. *It's all in my mind. A sham. I'm fine. Completely fine.*

Since I was maybe thirteen, compulsive thoughts have ruled my life. It could start as something simple—an itch on my head would spark thoughts of lice. Repeating thoughts would manifest into symptoms. Before long, I'd be itching for days on end like a maniac.

I wanted to think I was completely over my self-destructive thoughts, but I'd have been lying. Techniques I learned in therapy only went so far. The fact was I was always a second away from the misery of a panic attack.

Daniel took his bat bag out of the trunk first, then handed me mine.

I slammed the trunk. "I'm going to be your catcher this year. Nothing's gonna stop me. You know that, right?"

Daniel looped his arm through the strap on his bag. "I know you are. I'm counting on it."

The black bat felt electric in my hands. A snug batting helmet pressed comfortably on my ears. Grass flattened under my sneakers.

Adrenaline flowed, tension drained. There would be no panic attack now.

From inside the batting cage, I looked left and scanned the practice field in the distance. Dew glistened on the grass. A cool breeze kicked up infield sand.

Daniel slid an L-shaped metal gate in front of the pitching machine. Protection from comebackers.

"Ready?"

"Let's do it," I said, teeth gritted, my hands choking the bat handle.

From behind the pitching machine, Daniel picked a baseball out of a bucket. He dropped the ball into a groove on the machine. Two spinning rubber wheels sucked it up and spat it out straight at me.

I swung hard, my right wrist rolling over my left. The ball thudded against the plastic wallboard behind me. Shit.

The next pitch, I chopped into the black netting that surrounded Daniel and me.

"Hit with your hips." He held up another ball. "Use your buck forty and drive it."

I fanned at the next pitch. Slammed my bat on home plate.

"Relax. Bunt it," he said.

The ball shot out of the machine. I bunted. A near-perfect bunt.

"There you go. You control the ball. Pick a spot. Send it there."

"Bend over," I said.

He laughed.

Two and a half hours later, blisters marked my hands. My arms felt like jelly. Daniel had called it quits at the plate about an hour ago.

I danced the bat above my shoulder. "Last one. I'm *so* done."

He flipped the power switch on the machine. "Take your last one on the diamond. Versus me."

I smiled. "I'm taking you downtown."

"You're talking about in your car, right? Because no way you're touching my heat."

We shared a laugh.

After we returned the equipment to the shed, he took the mound on the practice field. I stepped up to the plate and waved the bat.

He lifted his cap, took a bow. "Ladies and gentlemen, your attention, please. On the mound for the New York Mets, number 39, Daniel Lembo." He cupped his hand over his mouth to mimic the sound of a roaring crowd.

"Let's go. Dad's going to lose it if I'm not back with the car by three."

He flashed an energetic grin. "I'll only need three pitches."

I squeezed the bat handle. "Just don't bean me."

He wound up. The ball hummed by me, my bat nearly flying out of my hands on my follow-through. "That's one," he said.

Holy heat. I should just start swinging before he throws it.

I whiffed at the next one, too. Not even close.

"That's two."

On the third pitch, he eased up. A lot. I punched the ball to right field.

"Nice shot," he said.

"My ass. You gave me a meatball."

He fetched the ball. "Just make sure you get your ass in the starting lineup. We have a no-hitter to work this year."

CHAPTER 7

THE BUS DRIVER, A BALD MAN WITH A NECK THAT SWELLED over his collar, locked his gaze on the big mirror above the windshield as my teammates and I filed in.

I slid into a seat four rows back. Daniel sat next to me.

After stowing my bat bag between my ankles, I held out my unsteady hands. "Look."

"Chill." Daniel tucked the front of his jersey into his baseball pants. "You can't screw up playing the bench."

I leaned forward, hugging myself. "My stomach doesn't feel right."

"You'll be fine."

I blew out a long breath. My bowels felt heavy, disturbed. All I needed now was to shit myself. I elbowed Daniel's arm. "Yo, I gotta hit the bathroom. Let me out."

"Dude, don't hold us up."

"Tell Coach I'll be right back."

Stepping off the bus, I raised a hand to shield my eyes from harsh sunrays.

Coach stood on the sidewalk, chatting on his cell.

"I'll be back in a sec," I said, jogging past him.

Coach pulled the phone away from his ear. "We leave in five."

I all but flew inside the school and to the bathroom stall. I threw down the lid, worked my jockstrap and baseball pants to my ankles and plopped down. My insides clenched. Sweat beaded on my forehead. A familiar feeling of misery overtook me.

After finishing up, I hustled back to the bus.

Seated in the first row, Coach stared at me as I entered the bus. I squeezed by Daniel's knees to reclaim the window seat.

From the back of the bus, Craig called out, "Guys, check it out. Coming at you, the Goody Shuffle."

Tommy Goodwin danced something funky down the narrow aisle.

Laughter echoed. Everybody seemed to be having a great time. Everybody except me.

Coach shook his head at Tommy's antics. "And you wonder why you're single."

The driver released the air brake, the school bus jerking into motion.

Daniel reached across the aisle and tapped Jerome's shoulder. "You ready?"

Jerome, a gangly black kid, removed his cap. Wiped his large hand over his shaved head. "Ready as I'll be. Wish I had your stuff."

"You'll do fine."

"Grovetown's 3 and 0. Every win by double digits."

"Don't forget, we're undefeated, too. Keep mixing it up. Throw some chin music. Back those suckers off the plate."

It seemed so easy for Daniel. So easy to talk to the guys. So easy to be cool. There were some guys on the team I hadn't spoken a single word to yet. My comfort zone was keeping quiet. Being as invisible as possible.

I put on my headphones and cranked up a Metallica song on my iPod. I stared out the window, and my thoughts shifted to batting practice. My awful performances on Monday and Tuesday. Soft hitting. Swings and misses. No dividends from the extra work I'd put in over the weekend. Coach couldn't have been impressed.

The bus rolled to a stop in the Grovetown parking lot. The yellow door clattered open. We shuffled out.

Dressed in blue and gray, the Grovetown Lions took fielding practice. They had more muscle-heads than the first two teams we faced. A lot more.

The starting lineup was taped to a backstop post. Coach had swapped Jerome and Craig's fielding positions. He put Daniel in right in place of Paul Winsor. Otherwise, it was a repeat of Friday's game.

Their ace, Eric Herman, stood atop the hill for Grovetown. His looks were made for a magazine cover. Tall and thin. Unblemished skin. Pearly white teeth. Light blond hair.

As if he didn't have enough going for him, the kid could throw. His warm-up pitches packed punch.

Pete knocked a doughnut-weight off his bat and studied the signs Coach flashed at him. Pete nodded and stepped up to the plate.

Herman wound up and lunged forward with his long legs. Pete took a wild swing. Strike one.

Herman needed five pitches to finish off Pete. The last one, a called strike on the outside corner.

Pete, storming toward the bench, launched his helmet into

the backstop. The ump pointed at Pete, then looked at Coach. "This is your warning. Another player throws equipment, they're ejected."

Pete muttered something. Coach's jaw bulged.

Two quick outs followed. Our starters took the field to warm up.

A short, stocky kid touched the tip of his bat to the corner of home plate. Nathan tapped his pencil on the scorebook. "This guy's good. Derrick Sadri. I remember him from JV last year."

I leaned forward and gripped the bench. "By the looks of these guys, Jerome's got his work cut out."

Nathan nodded.

Jerome hurled a belt-high fastball. Sadri dropped a bunt down the third base line. Tommy Goodwin raced in and grabbed it, but he had no play versus the speedy leadoff batter.

Working out of the stretch, Jerome eyed the runner taking an aggressive lead.

"He's going," I said. "Bet you."

And Sadri did break for second. Joey caught the inside strike, double-clutched, then chucked the ball over Mike Kane's head. Craig rushed in, his glove low to the ground. He scooped up the ball and fired it on a bounce to Tommy at third. A split-second late.

Jerome fanned the second batter. Walked the third.

The cleanup hitter, Mattelson, lumbered up to home plate. Veins swelled on his large forearms. Broad shoulders swallowed his thick neck.

"What's in the water at Grovetown?" I asked. "These guys are huge."

Nathan leaned forward. "This guy's an all-county nose tackle. No joke."

Jerome locked on the target Joey set. He rocked into

motion, hurled a low fastball. The batter swung under it, popped it sky-high to left. Pete drifted back and squeezed it.

The runners tagged: 1-0. First time we'd been down this season.

By the time Dad showed up in the third inning, Grovetown was up 6-0.

Our bats stayed asleep until the fifth. That was when Jake blasted a solo shot over the right-field fence. The rally didn't have legs, though. Tommy and Craig followed with whiffs.

Jerome's struggles continued in the bottom half of the fifth, walking the inning's leadoff batter on four straight. And just as Grovetown had been doing all game, the base runner went on the first pitch. Joey had no answer, again, bouncing an offline throw to second base.

Color rising in his face, Coach strode toward the benchwarmers. He looked at me.

Shit.

"Lembo. Next inning. Catcher."

My fingertips tingled. "Okay."

"Joey'll bat if he comes up the top half of the inning."

I nodded, unable to breathe. Coach walked away.

Nathan slugged my arm. "Told you, man. Told you."

"Holy crap." I glanced over my shoulder at Dad. My stomach did that flipping thing. "Wanna throw?"

"Sure."

Usually, throwing calmed me. Not today. My palms were puddles. I shivered. Felt lightheaded, weak at the knees.

Dad worked his way down the bleachers over to Nathan and me in foul territory. "They're a tough team."

I picked Nathan's throw out of the dirt. "Yeah. I'm going in next inning."

Dad folded his arms. "Really? Well, good. Can't let a team like this run at will."

I snapped the ball to Nathan. "I'll do my best."

"Good luck." Dad returned to his seat next to Uncle John and Aunt Sue.

It was amazing what baseball did to the man. He couldn't be bothered with me when I was a cut-from-the-team loser. Put a uniform on me, and he acted like we were regular buds.

On the field, Jerome worked himself out of a base-loaded jam, no runs tacked on.

I caught Nathan's throw, then pulled off my glove. "I'm good."

Coach met up with Joey by the backstop. I couldn't make out the conversation, but it was one-sided. All Coach. Joey nodded several times. Coach walked away and Joey lingered by the backstop.

I'd been keeping my distance from him since joining the team, but I screwed up courage and walked over to him.

"Nice game," I said.

"Fuck you." He snapped off a shin guard.

My body went rigid. "Huh?"

"You heard me."

"Where'd that come from?"

He ducked out of his chest protector. "Cut means cut."

"Coach asked me to come back on the team."

"Right. Just Coach. Don't you have a shrink session to go to or something?"

"What's your problem?"

The vein on Joey's temple pulsed. "Haven't you even noticed?"

"Noticed?"

"Yeah, that nobody talks to you, or wants you and that freaky face of yours on the team. Except, maybe, your family."

A switch went off. Nervousness gave way to raw anger. "Enjoy the bench."

He got in my face, a flash of fire in his eyes. "Better watch what you say to me. And, yes, that's a threat."

My heart hammering, I stepped away. This wasn't the time or place. I needed to focus on the game. To make sure Joey didn't get a chance to get back in the lineup.

He found a spot on the bench. I dumped the equipment bag, my mind scrambling.

Daniel strutted toward me and lowered his hand. "Nathan just told me. Sweet news."

I turned away, not feeling like celebrating.

He caught my shoulder, spun me toward him. "What, now you too good for our handshake?"

I looked directly into his green eyes. "Just leave me alone."

"Whatever," he said, a hard edge to his voice.

I turned my back to him again. This time he walked away.

I squatted behind home plate and adjusted my cup.

Jerome motioned me to the mound.

Jeez.

I flipped my mask up and ran out to him, rattled, unfocused.

Jerome tucked his glove under his arm, rubbed down the ball. "Damn, kid. You just go back there, say nothing?"

"Sorry."

"Let's use two fingers as the indicator. Next sign is what I'll throw. One fast. Two curve. Three change."

"Sounds good."

Jerome slapped my forearm with his mitt. "Don't look so damn excited."

"Yeah." I pulled my mask over my face. Jogged back to the plate.

As warm-up pitches pounded into my mitt, the ump confirmed the score with both sides: 6-1, Grovetown.

"Batter up," the ump called out.

Sardi settled into a stance. The corners, Tommy and Jake, played in to guard against a bunt.

Down in the crouch, I flashed signs between my legs. Two fingers, then one. I shifted to the inside half of the plate. Held my mitt steady.

Jerome wound up. Sardi squared to bunt then pulled back as the pitch bounced in the dirt. I blocked it with my chest protector.

He swung at the next pitch, bouncing it to short. Mike charged in, but the ball squirted under his glove. It would have been a tough play even if he had fielded it cleanly.

My body a coiled spring, I shifted my gaze to where Sadri was taking a sizable lead off first. I gritted my teeth. Curled my right hand into a tight fist behind my back.

Jerome lifted his left leg. The runner went. Already coming out of the chute, I caught the inside strike and slung a dart to second. The throw arrived low to the bag, right into Kevin's waiting glove. A bang-bang play. Kevin showed the ump the ball. The ump punched air.

"Atta boy, Andy," Coach called out.

Teammate cheers echoed.

I socked my mitt. *Chew on that, Joey.*

The third out came on a line drive that Jake Murphy lunged to snag. A scoreless inning.

As I peeled off gear, a few of the guys praised my play. I wondered if Joey was full of shit, if he was the only one with something against me.

Daniel swaggered toward me, his hand in position for our handshake. "Don't dis me again."

I cracked a smile. We did our handshake. Low fives. A sideways chest bump.

"Awesome throw, dude. That kid's lightning and you nailed him."

"Now it's your turn. Start a rally."

Daniel picked up a helmet off the ground. "You know it."

I checked the posted lineup. Joey made the final out last inning. Odds were I wouldn't have to bat this game. Especially with the way Grovetown had silenced our bats.

I sat next to Nathan on the bench. "Great play, man."

"Thanks." I smoothed my hands on my legs, pushing myself straighter.

"Seventh inning. Last chance, guys," Nathan called out. "Daniel, then the top of the order."

Daniel got into his batting stance. Twirled the bat. If he was nervous, it didn't show.

The first pitch came in ankle low. He chased it, chipping a shot that landed between the shortstop and left fielder.

I clapped. "Yeah, Daniel. C'mon, we can do this!"

Pete singled, too, advancing Daniel to third base. Mike followed with a walk. The bases were loaded with Panthers.

Jake, our team's best hitter, stared down the pitcher, twisted his hands around the bat handle, forearms flexing.

Herman brought the heat. Jake blasted a ball that had the distance to leave the park, but it sliced foul.

Two consecutive curve balls buckled Jake's knees. Back to the bench he went.

"Time to bring home the ducks," Tommy said, flapping his arms.

Tommy got behind in the count, 0 and 2.

Herman shook off the catcher's sign. Then nodded. He threw a hanging curve. Tommy sat back on it and launched a missile over the left-field fence. A grand salami: 6-5, Grovetown.

I pumped my fist. "Yeah, baby! Yeah!" My body buzzed with excitement.

Tommy paraded around the bases. I joined the guys by home plate to congratulate him.

Tommy received me with a high five. "We're in this game. Let's go."

Craig rolled up his sleeves. Grabbed a green bat off the rack. "They better back up. That's all I'm saying."

Daniel patted Craig on the butt. "Do it, kid."

Craig took a homerun swing at Eric's first pitch. Strike one. The next pitch handcuffed him, but Craig was able to muscle it into left field for a base hit.

The Grovetown coach had seen enough. He pulled Herman and brought in a lean kid with straight black hair. "Jose Cruz, 43, is replacing Eric Herman, 16," the ump said to Nathan.

"Okay, got it," Nathan replied.

I walked over to Nathan. "I'm on double deck, right?"

"You sure are."

My throat tightened. I lifted my cap, pushed up my bangs. "Great."

"Your chance to be a hero."

"Or a zero."

I went behind the backstop, popped on a helmet and took practice swings. I studied Cruz's delivery. Short and compact. Seemed to telegraph his curve by dropping his elbow.

It was Jerome's turn to keep the rally alive, to help his cause. He took a good hack at the first pitch but came up empty. Behind in the count, he ended up chasing a bad pitch and popping it up. Two outs.

My stomach grumbled. I could hardly watch.

Kevin stepped up to the plate, poised and focused. He worked the count full, hitting foul ball after foul ball. Then Cruz bounced a fastball in the dirt. Ball four.

Oh, boy.

The crowd stood. The teams stood. Nervous cheers echoed.

I took slow steps toward the plate.

"Andy," Daniel called out.

I looked at him.

He held out a clenched fist. "You got this, bro. A hit ties it up."

I nodded.

Coach flashed me the take sign. No surprise there.

I stepped into the box, my body shaking. *Please walk me. Please.*

Cruz focused in on the catcher. He wound up. His fastball bounced, scooted past the catcher. Craig and Kevin advanced a base.

Throw another one away. Just one more for the tie.

But Cruz threw me a perfect pitch. Strike one.

Shit. My shaking intensified.

Cruz worked quick, hurling a letter-high fastball. During my swing and miss, the bat slipped out of my hand and finally stopped flipping and rolling by the shortstop.

A chorus of laughter.

My face flushed.

*Why, God? Why?

I met the shortstop halfway. He handed me the bat.

"Hey, Lembo," Joey called out. "Put some glue on those hands."

I pretended not to hear him.

Standing outside the batter's box, I drew a breath. Exhaled slowly. *This is it. Down to my last strike.*

I stepped in the box, steeled myself.

Throw a wild pitch. Please.

Cruz rocked into motion and hurled a knee-high fastball. My bat on my shoulder, I looked back at the ump.

"Strike three."

No.

Craig slammed his helmet in the dirt. "Damn!"

I blinked hard, wanting to disappear. I stepped out of the box, my head down.

"Shake it off, kid," Coach said, walking toward me. "Get 'em next time."

I nodded, a lump swelling in my throat.

I risked a glance at Dad. He was on his way to the parking lot, his back to me. Nice.

Daniel dropped a hand on my shoulder. "Nothing you could do. He threw you a tough one."

"Yeah. I suck."

"We all hit like crap today."

Water glazed my eyes. "I lost the game for the team."

"Did not. C'mon, let's shake hands with them."

CHAPTER 8

I PULLED A SWEATSHIRT OVER MY JERSEY AND SAT ON THE bench in front of my locker. Coach walked in and closed the door behind him.

I bit my lower lip, hoping he wouldn't single me out.

Coach's eyes scanned the players changing. "I'm not going to sugarcoat the loss. Yes, we came back. But we need to play hard for seven innings. Seven goddamn innings. I can accept the physical errors. They're part of the game. What I won't accept are the mental mistakes. The lazy play. You run everything out. Everything! We need to start playing as a team. I want everyone on their feet when we're hitting. Starting tomorrow, we'll run the school's perimeter before practice."

A few groans.

"And we'll keep that up till we can show a seven-inning effort worthy of our rating. Latest polls before today's game have us ranked at the top of our league. Fourth in the state. Hungry teams will be gunning for us."

He flicked up the brim of his hat. "I know the talent's here to do big things this year. But talent alone isn't enough." He thumped his chest. "Here's where you'll find it. Deep inside."

He pursed his lips, nostrils flaring. "That's all. Have a g'night, guys. Get home safe."

After he left, Craig stood. "The school's perimeter? Dudes, you better start hustling your asses off. I'm not running that every practice."

Joey spun his hat backwards then took a Wiffle Ball and plastic yellow bat out of his locker. He flipped the ball to Craig. "Shut up, drama queen, and pitch me one."

"Oh, snap. I'm a Wiffle Ball legend," Craig said. He peered at the locker room door like it was an imaginary catcher.

Craig pitched. Joey swung and missed, letting go of his bat mid-swing. The bat rolled to Pete's feet. The entire team broke out in laughter.

Joey looked at me and winked. I forced a smile, my cheeks burning.

Daniel scooped up the Wiffle Ball and tossed it to Craig. "Give it here," Daniel said, crouching down, holding out his hand as if it were a catcher's mitt.

"Watch the break on this one," Craig said, winding up.

Daniel caught his pitch and called out, "He's going." Then he threw the ball so high that it hit the ceiling.

More laughter. Everyone except me.

"You got me. My last throw did suck." Joey walked over and gave Daniel a high five.

"Seriously, guys," Daniel said. "Let's live up to the hype."

I just wanted to go home. It was my fault we were no longer undefeated. Mine.

The high beams from Craig's car lit up the back of my Corolla. Well, Dad's Corolla now.

Daniel and I hopped out of the car.

"Later, guys." Daniel gave a quick wave.

"Peace." Craig backed his car out of the driveway and floored it down the road.

Crickets chirped. A cool breeze bent trees. "I cost the team the game," I said.

Daniel shook his head. "Are you really going to dwell on this? Let it go."

"Joey has it in for me. It's like he's ready to kick my ass or something."

Daniel laughed. "Stop. The Wiffle bat thing was a joke. It was actually pretty funny."

I dropped my bat bag and folded my arms. "He said nobody wants me on the team. Me and my ugly face."

Daniel's face went limp. "He said that?"

"Right after Coach pulled him."

He waved my comment away. "Just ignore him. You saw how excited everyone was for you when you pegged that guy at second. Play good, and keep his ass on the bench. I have a hunch Coach is going to start you next game. Joey can't handle my heat. You're used to it."

"Joey got two hits today."

"Doesn't matter."

"Doubt it."

We went inside. Dad sat on his recliner, his eyes on the TV. I kicked off my sneakers in the foyer, tension gripping at my neck muscles. Daniel walked into the living room and sat on the couch.

Dad stood abruptly and brushed salt off his sweatpants. "What happened today, Andy?"

I drew up my shoulders. "I don't know. Just messed up, I guess."

"The pressure got to you. You need to stay cool up there. Like Daniel."

"I'm not Daniel. In case you haven't noticed."

Dad coughed. "Don't be a smartass."

The plastic on the couch crackled as Daniel stood. "Dad—"

"Save it," Dad said, his hand extended like a crossing guard. "Andy, you'll have your car back Friday."

"You sold the bat?" I asked in a clipped tone.

"No. Your aunt was looking to trade in her Malibu. We worked something out."

I nodded. "Cool."

Dad rubbed his neck. "One more thing. Any interest in going to a Mets game April 30th?"

Daniel shook my shoulder, knocking me off balance. "Hell yeah."

A smile bent the lines in Dad's face. "Uncle John offered. He has a ticket plan, invited us to go with him."

"Nice," Daniel said.

"I'm down," I said.

"I'll let him know. Cold cuts are in the fridge."

Daniel and I hadn't been to a pro game in years. Back when the Mets played at Shea Stadium. Back when Dad wasn't such a dick.

Thanks to Coach working us longer than usual at practice, I was running at least twenty minutes late for my evening therapy session with Dr. Steward. I hustled toward her office, my sneakers squeaking on the shiny main lobby floor. I arrived at her closed door, exhaled, and knocked.

"You're not going to find her in there," a man's voice chimed from behind me.

"Oh, she left?" I asked, turning toward the guy.

He approached me, loosening his necktie, a briefcase active at his side. "Medics came early this morning. Took her out on a stretcher."

"No. What happened? She okay?"

His gaze was steady on my scar. "Not sure. Sorry."

I folded my arms and felt my right bicep spasm. "Do you happen to know which hospital?"

"I think someone said St. Catherine of Siena."

St. Catherine of Siena.

A few years ago, Aunt Sue had a brief stay at that hospital, some kind of infection. Dad, Daniel, and I were vacationing downstate at the time. Naturally, we went to visit her. Big mistake. I quickly went from a visitor to a patient. Panic attack. A bad one that left me passed out beside the nurse's station. Just before I lost consciousness, I remembered gasping for air, the hospital walls closing in on me. For whatever reason, being inside that hospital, even just walking through the main doors, triggered intense thoughts of the day the Bitch went crazy with the iron. Punishing images of the emergency room rescue scene, my face bloodied, my two-year-old world collapsed.

The muscles in my neck tensing, I thanked the man for letting me know about Dr. Steward.

He gave me a sideways glance. "Hey, aren't you on my son Joey's baseball team?"

Joey's dad. Of course. The resemblance was suddenly clear. I forgot that his office was down the hall from Dr. Steward's.

"Um, yeah. Same team."

We chatted a bit then said our goodbyes. He walked off, a strut to his step.

I leaned back against the door to my doctor's office and

pictured medical staff storming past me and finding Dr. Steward on her office floor, her body curled in the fetal position, her face bent in agony.

Did she have a stroke?

A seizure?

My heartbeat seemed off and I coughed into my closed fist.

I could be next. Heart failure's in my bloodline.

Stop it, Andy.

On rubbery legs, I trekked across the hall and entered the men's room. Lights burned bright, the mirror revealing the true deformity of my face. I claimed an open stall and sat on the bowl, sweatpants still up. My breath uneven, I removed my baseball cap and dragged my fingers through my sweaty hair. I imagined Dr. Steward in pain, dying.

Even though we only met once, I had connected with her. She was kind in a way that couldn't be faked. Her concern for me seemed genuine. A concern I wanted to return. But hospitals rattled me. Especially that one.

I stood up, pressed my hands against the stall door, and whispered, "I have to stop this. I have to stop letting fear control me."

I parked in the hospital's visitor section, my thumbnails deepening grooves in the steering wheel. I mostly wanted to go home. But a smaller, usually quieter, part of me was tired of my fears having the final say. It was a personal challenge now. I was going to make this happen, or pass out trying.

A siren blared. Flashing lights winked through the trees on the road leading the hospital. An ambulance charged into sight and turned sharply into the emergency entrance.

Craig crashed his car.

Daniel's hurt.

Stop it, Andy.

Stop it.

An accident scene popped into my mind. Craig's car pancaked, twisted metal and shattered glass everywhere. Daniel on the stretcher, unresponsive, his face soaked with blood.

Stop it.

I'm in control of my thoughts.

Me.

The sensible thing to do was retreat to my car. Give myself a break from the anxiety. But I dug deep and pressed on. Down a walkway I went, past the general entrance to the hospital. A safe distance away, I watched medical staff back a stretcher out of the ambulance. A man, eightyish, lay on it, an oxygen mask strapped over his face.

See, Andy.

Not Daniel.

Just an old man.

My tension eased a little. I trekked on, back up the path and into the hospital through the main entrance. A full-figured woman at the information desk told me where I could find Mary Steward. Room 314. The cardiac floor.

I marched on, knowing I had an out if things got bad. I could just turn around and leave. Nobody expected me to be there.

Air whistling through my pinched lips, I battled a siege of twisted thoughts in the elevator and past the nurses' station. Thoughts that took me down years earlier.

I arrived at Room 314, bent the brim on baseball cap, and peeked in.

"Andy," Dr. Steward said, her bed tilted upright, a novel in her hand. "What a nice surprise."

I inched in and stood rigidly. The bed next to her was empty, the curtain fully open. Machines beeped. A bag dripped clear fluid. Monitors above her bed displayed her vitals.

"How are you?" I choked out.

Dr. Steward set the book down and folded her veiny hands over her chest. "I'm just fine. Which is what I keep telling the doctors. I had a little false alarm. Some pain in my chest. They want a full workup on me to make sure everything's okay. Which I guess is a good thing."

The calm tone of her voice worked like magic to ease my tension. "Oh. You seem to be in good spirits. I know your patients aren't supposed to show up here, but—"

"No, it's fine. I love the company. My family has been here most of the day. They just went out to get a bite to eat. They'll be back shortly."

Her family photos were arranged on the windowsill. "I don't want to be a bother. I'll get going and let you get your rest."

"You're no bother. Why not sit and let's chat a bit?"

"I, um. Sure." I sat in the plastic chair beside her bed.

She nudged her bifocals up on her nose. "Didn't you tell me hospitals were one of your triggers?"

I looked down and scrubbed my hands over my thighs. "Yeah. A panic attack happened a few years ago at this very hospital, actually. The fifth floor."

"I'm sorry that happened to you. But look at you now. Showing up here and showing your fear who's boss. I'm impressed."

"Thanks. I'm not out of the woods yet. And I don't really want this visit to be about me. You're the one with all those wires stuck to you."

She smiled. "I'd like to stop thinking about me in this place for a bit. This isn't a session. This is two people talking. That's it."

"Cool. I like that."

"But if I could ask just one psychologist-type question." Her eyebrows went high. "How's your anxiety right now?"

I sucked my lips in. "A seven out of ten, I guess. My mind keeps wanting to take me back to that day. The bloody emergency room. Y'know, I wasn't supposed to make it. Doctors almost didn't save me."

"But they did. They did save you, Andy. You survived that day for a reason. And the reason isn't to be tormented by that day. It's to rise above it. It's to live your life on your terms."

I looked at the wavelengths flowing on the monitor. "And you survived today for a reason too, right?"

"That's right. I have a decent-sized bucket list. Like seeing the weddings of my grandchildren. Going to Paris. And helping my wonderfully brave and kind clients. How about you? Any bucket list?"

My thoughts shifted to baseball and my tension eased. "Winning the high school baseball championship with my brother would be nice. Maybe the two of us working a perfect game. Oh, snap. I didn't tell you. I'm back playing ball with my bro."

"Fantastic. Good for you, Andy. I hope you guys do win that championship."

"Thanks."

Her face went serious. "You know, time moves slower in a hospital. I end up thinking a lot. Deep thoughts. I think about the good things in my life, like my family. But I also think about regrets. Luckily, I don't have too many of those. The best advice an old bat like me can give to young folks is to go for it. Whatever *it* is. Live with no regrets."

"That's real good advice," I said. And really, it was.

Her family walked in, a dozen of them, toddlers to elders.

I stood up.

"Everybody, this is Andy. My good friend."

They greeted me.

I smiled. "I was just leaving. Nice to meet all of you."

"Take care, Andy," Dr. Steward said, her lips twisting into a smile.

"Feel better." I know I already did.

CHAPTER 9

THE SCHOOL CAFETERIA ECHOED WITH CHATTER. I BIT into a slice of pizza, the cheese stretching as I pulled it away.

Some of my tablemates talked about the *Titanic*, a topic that interested me zero. I said nothing, thinking about practice. About Joey.

I glanced over my shoulder at the wall clock. Hailey Baye twirled her index finger through her blonde hair. Her mouth was drawn up, eyes flirty. I'd say she was checking me out if I didn't know better. But girls in her league don't flirt with me. No girls in any league, actually.

I studied my pizza and thought about what Dr. Steward said at the hospital. *Go for it. Live with no regrets.* I risked a glance back at her. She flashed a smile at me. I looked away, tiny prickles detonating all over my skin.

I allowed myself to dream. Hailey and Andy. Beauty and the Beast.

As I folded my pizza slice and opened my trap, someone poked my shoulder.

"Andy, right?" Hailey asked.

Nodding, I nearly swallowed my tongue.

"Can I sit for a second?"

The guys' jaws hung loose. "Sure." I brushed sweaty palms on the sides of my pants. "S-sit."

She took the chair next to me, her legs squeezed by my jeans. My heart knocked like a shoe in a dryer. *Don't say anything stupid. Please. Just this once.*

She leaned forward, cleavage showing. "I hear you're Daniel's brother."

My shoulders slumped forward. Of course. Daniel. "Yep."

"I saw him pitch. He's unbelievable."

"Yeah, great," I said.

"Does he have a girlfriend?"

"No."

She slid a piece of paper in front of me. "Ask him to give me a call if he wants. Hailey."

"Will do."

She stood. "Thanks. Sorry to interrupt, guys."

Then she was gone.

"Jeez," Mark said. "The hottest girl in the school just sat at our table."

"I know," Ralph said, beating his forehead. "Thought I was gonna crap myself."

Nathan leaned back, his hands laced behind his head. "Your brother's a god among peasants. Hailey Baye. Unbelievable."

Daniel flicked on the bedroom light and perched on the edge of his bed. After placing my bat bag on my dresser, I sat on my bed, across from him. "C'mon. Call her already."

He stared down at his cell phone, his legs shaking. "I don't know. What the hell am I going to say?"

"Ask her how her day was. Ask her to go to the movies this weekend. I can drive."

"What movie?"

"Dude, just call. Do you know how many people would give their left nut to be in your position?"

He dialed, his lips pressed tight. "It's ringing." A second later, he snapped his phone shut. "No, I'm way too nervous."

I leaned forward, snatched the phone out of his hand. "Give it back," he barked.

I switched the phone to speaker, hit redial.

"Yo, give me it," Daniel said louder, clawing my arm.

"Hello," Hailey said.

I sat next to him, motioning him to talk.

"Hey, Hailey. It's, um, Daniel."

"Hey, there. Guess your brother gave you my number."

"Um, yeah." He shrugged as though she could see him. "He did."

She giggled. "You're some pitcher. How do you throw that ball so hard?"

Red suffused Daniel's face. "I don't know."

Awkward silence.

I whispered in his ear, "Ask about her."

"So, do you play any sports?"

"Gymnastics."

"Oh, wow. What event you best at?"

"Hmm. I'd say the balance beam."

"Cool. I probably couldn't make it across."

"Sure you could."

More awkward silence.

"When do you pitch next?"

"Tomorrow. An away game."

"Aww, I wish I could see it. Good luck."

"Thanks."

He looked at me, drew his shoulders up. I mouthed, "Ask her out."

"Umm," his voice cracked. "Maybe this Saturday night we can do something. You like the movies?"

More giggles. "Sure I do."

"I mean, we can do something else. Mini golf. Bowling. You name it."

"It doesn't matter. Have you been to Adventureland?"

"No. What's that?"

"An amusement park. It's about twenty minutes away. Might be a fun time."

"Sounds it. I, uh, don't have my license yet. Andy said he'd chauffeur."

"Oh, okay. Would you mind if I asked my friend Lisa Grant to tag along? You know, for Andy?"

Lisa Grant. Plump and chirpy. I sucked in air, shook my head like a wet puppy.

He socked my arm. "Sure. Definitely."

"Great. Wish I could talk more, but I have to go. Can you give me a call tomorrow and let me know how the game went?"

"Sure. Will do."

"Great. Strike 'em all out."

He laughed. "I'll try. Goodnight, Hailey."

"Goodnight. Bye."

I leaned forward, pulled at my hair. "Jeez. Lisa Grant? She has to be like two hundred and fifty pounds!"

He clapped my back. "Stop. She's got a cute face. Maybe

she'll be a knockout once she decides to shed the extra pounds. Anyway, it's what's on the inside that counts, right, champ?"

"Easy for you to say. You get Hailey. Lisa will probably say no anyway. I mean, look at me."

"Stop. We're going on a double date. Your first date. This calls for a handshake, bro."

I stood. "You're an ass."

We shook, capping it with a chest bump.

The Lindenhurst Bulldogs, in blue and white uniforms, warmed up with jumping jacks on the sunlit outfield grass. They hadn't won a game all season, but they'd been in each game. No blowouts.

I sat on our bench on the third-base side and changed into cleats, concentrating on each breath. In through the nose, out through the mouth.

After we stretched, threw, and took fielding practice, Coach called us in. Two scouts set up camp behind the backstop. I jogged in and joined my teammates over by our bench.

Coach spit sunflower shells. "Let's play hard. Just like we practiced yesterday." He turned his scorebook over. "Here's the lineup we'll go with. Andy'll lead us off and catch. Pete …"

He went on, but I couldn't process what he was saying. Daniel squeezed my arm.

"Let's go," Coach said. "All hands in."

On three, we screamed, "Panthers."

"Lead off, bro," Daniel said, then dropped a hand on my shoulder and added, "and my catcher."

I stiffened. Cut my gaze to home plate. "Battery brothers."

He shook my shoulder. "You know it."

"Andy, here," Coach motioned me over by the field. I jogged toward him.

He hitched at his belt. "Ready to show me what you're made of?"

I nodded.

"Start us up, kid."

I went behind the backstop and popped on a helmet. After selecting a bat, I slid a doughnut weight on it.

Joey walked past me. "Don't choke."

I took warm-up swings, unfazed. My mind was focused on leading off. On catching my little brother. On playing the game I love.

The Bulldogs' pitcher, Sam O'Reilly, got loose on the mound. A sidearmer, his warm-up pitches lacked the fire of his red hair.

The field stretched an acre deep, bordered by a playground and a forest of pines. No home-run fence. I found Aunt Sue and Uncle John amongst the fans. Not Dad.

"Batter up," the ump called out.

I strode to the batter's box but stopped a few feet from it. I turned and met Coach's gaze.

Standing by the third base coach's box, Coach flashed a few fake signs. Then he pinched his ear and swiped his hand across chest. Bunt.

"Let's go, Andy," Daniel called out. "Drive one."

I turned to Daniel and my other teammates, all standing behind a chain-link fence. Some joined Daniel's lead and cheered me on.

I stepped up to the plate. Composed. In the zone.

The pitcher, standing atop the hill pawed at his freckled face. He gave his catcher a quick nod.

I tightened my grip on the bat. As he wound up, I squared to bunt.

The pitch came in low, but I put metal to it. Pushed a slow roller to the third-base side of the field. My head down, I motored to first. As I overran the bag, the ball popped into the first baseman's glove. Safe. Cheers echoed. My body buzzed with excitement.

I placed a foot on the base, studied Coach's signs. Steal.

Taking a healthy lead off first, I wiggled my hands in front of my kneecaps.

The pitcher stepped off the rubber and snapped a throw to the first baseman.

I dove back to the bag in time. I stood and brushed myself off.

When O'Reilly rocked into motion, I took off. Dirt moving under me. But Pete fouled off the pitch.

I jogged back to first.

Coach gave me the steal sign again.

I widened my lead.

As the pitcher started his windup, I broke. Arms pumping hard, I took flight, dove headfirst into second. The tag came late. More cheers.

Breathing hard and fast, I called for a time out.

"Atta way, kid," Coach said, his voice deep.

Pete settled into a batting stance, nice and compact.

Taking a conservative lead, I threw a glance at the second baseman, then back to O'Reilly.

Pete battled the pitcher to a full count. Then O'Reilly's letter-high fastball overpowered him. Strike three.

Pete and Jake knocked knuckles as they swapped spots.

Jake turned on Sam's first pitch, a flat fastball. The ball exploded off the bat, skipped into right field.

I sprinted toward third, and Coach's arm whirled. "Go, go, go!"

I rounded third, floored it home.

The first baseman cut off the right fielder's throw.

I crossed home plate, my adrenaline surging. One to nothing.

I received high fives, helmet slaps. Daniel jogged toward me, grinning. "Yeah, bro."

I chest bumped him. "There's the run you need."

"No doubt."

I bowled my helmet into the backstop. Stoked. High on the game.

Before O'Reilly retired our side, we tacked on another three runs.

In catcher's gear, I shadowed Daniel to the mound, picked up the game ball, and smacked it into Daniel's glove. "We always dreamed of this."

Daniel tipped up his cap. Sucked in his lips. "Since grade school. Same signs?"

"Yep. Let's go. Make my glove pop." I flipped my mask down.

"Yo, look who made it." He shifted his gaze into foul territory.

Dad walked with purpose down a hill leading to the bleachers, his left hand raised to shield sunlight as he looked out at us.

"That's him." I walked back behind the plate, got in position. Daniel's warm-up pitches hummed and snapped my mitt back.

Lindenhurst's leadoff batter, a featherweight, touched the tip of his metal bat to home plate.

I gave signs between my legs. Shifted toward the outer half of the plate.

Daniel nodded. I held a steady target.

He wound up, threw smoke down the middle.

"Whoa," the hitter muttered, the bat on his shoulder. I zipped the ball back to Daniel.

The batter watched the next two pitches blow by him. I stood and gunned the ball down to Tommy at third. The infielders completed throwing the ball around the horn.

Daniel overwhelmed the next batter, too.

The Lindenhurst Bulldogs cheered on their number-three hitter, Charlie, a southpaw with an athletic build and a pinched face. He dragged a bunt down the first-base line. Jake raced in, scooped it, and tried to swipe a tag, but Charlie was already by him.

"No sweat. Get the next guy." I walked back to the plate adjusting my mask.

"My bad. Shit," Daniel said.

Daniel kept the runner close, tossing a couple over to first to keep him honest.

On a 1–1 count, Charlie broke for second. I caught the inside strike and skipped the ball to Kevin, who picked it and slapped a tag on the runner. Inning over.

"Yeah!" I clenched my fist. "Nice play, Kev."

Daniel slapped my butt. "Sweet throw."

As I made my way to the bench, Nathan, Pete, and others congratulated me. Not Joey. Not that I expected him to.

"Way to bring it, Andy," Coach said. "Good job."

Snapping off my shin guard, I smiled. It had to be the best moment I'd experienced since we moved to Collingwood.

"Wahoo! Way to go, Andy," Aunt Sue called out from the bleachers.

I raised my hand, acknowledging her.

Dad, seated next to Aunt Sue, pointed at me. I pointed back.

Daniel grabbed a helmet for himself and tossed me one.

"Start a rally," I said.

"Yeah, I hate sidearmers."

While I stood on deck, Daniel readied himself at the plate.

He let two outside pitches go by.

"Let's go, Daniel," I said. "Pick one out."

He crowded the plate. O'Reilly's pitch tailed inside and plunked him on his thigh.

"Hey, watch it, freckles," Craig called out.

Daniel stared at the pitcher for a second then flipped his bat over to me, jogged to first base. Didn't rub his leg. Not once.

I handed Daniel's bat to Pete. Then I walked out to the field, studying Coach. I expected him to give me the bunt sign. He didn't. I tightened my face, waved the bat. Focused on driving the ball back up the middle.

The first two pitches went by high and outside, both balls. I locked onto his next pitch, slicing it to right field.

Stay fair. Stay fair.

The ball landed just inside the foul line.

The first-base coach yelled for me to go. Rounding first, I flicked a glance at the outfielder chasing the ball, which had scooted past him.

Coach waved me to third. I went for it like a raging bull.

Daniel scored.

Sucking wind, I stopped at third.

"Nice shot," Coach said.

Daniel dealt teammates a round of high fives. Dad whistled. Aunt Sue hooted. Uncle John clapped. "Yeah, Andy," Nathan called out.

My lips flirted with a smile as I took it all in.

Pete, behind in the count, skied O'Reilly's pitch to deep right. After the fielder reined it in, I tagged up and scored without a throw: 5-0.

We added another run in the second inning then broke the game open in the top of the fourth: 14-0. Mercy-rule territory, which meant Lindenhurst would need to score at least two runs in their half of the fourth inning to keep the game alive.

I squatted behind the plate, waiting for Daniel to get his butt to the mound and warm-up. Joey walked past me. "Wow. Your looks really improve with that mask on."

I looked away, wanting to tell him to shove it. But I couldn't find the courage, so I let it go.

Joey jogged out to right field, his glove tucked under his arm. Coach made some lineup changes. Sent in a few bench players to do mop-up work.

Daniel picked up the game ball off the grass and climbed the mound. I blew out a breath, struggling to keep my mind on the game. On the gem Daniel and I were working.

He struck out the first two batters, even though he was easing up on the hitters. He didn't even appear to be trying. But it didn't matter. He was in a league of his own. A bunt hit, a dink single, and a few walks was all the offense Lindenhurst was able to muster.

Daniel nodded at my fastball sign. He kicked up his leg, hurled low heat. The batter chipped it, a popup behind the second base bag. Kevin circled under the ball and squeezed it.

I flipped off my mask, ran out to Daniel and gave him a high five.

"Nice game," I said.

He wrapped his arm around my shoulder. "You played great, bro. We'll get that no-hitter. Someday."

CHAPTER 10

DANIEL STUNK WITH COLOGNE. HE'D TUCKED A GOLD cross necklace under his T-shirt collar.

I stepped into a pair of khaki pants. Sat on the edge of my bed. Choking down vomit. The same vomit I'd been swallowing for an hour now.

"You going on rides?" he asked.

"I don't do roller coasters."

"Wimp. Guess somebody has to hold the girls' purses."

I made a face. "You gonna reach first base with Hailey?"

He squeezed gel from a tube onto his fingertips, poked at his hair. "Count on it. Bet Lisa'll give you a big wet one."

"Shut up."

When we were done primping, I dogged him into the kitchen. Then I detoured out the back door and jogged to a wooded area of the yard. Found a bush. Puked hard and fast. Coughed. Wiped my mouth with the back of my hand.

I squeezed my eyes shut. Colored dots floated in the darkness. I hoped Dad didn't see me through the kitchen window. To him, anxiety was a character flaw. A weakness. He had no clue. None.

Yesterday, I was actually looking forward to tonight. To putting an end to my lifelong dateless streak. But now it didn't seem worth the trouble.

Bent over, I spat on the dirt. I straightened up and trekked back to the house, stomach gargling, emptied and raw. I entered through the back door.

Dad closed the fridge, forced his gaze at me. "Why's the garbage still sitting there?"

"Relax. I'll take it out."

His forehead creased. "Don't tell me to relax."

"Fine."

"Is your room picked up?"

"My side is," Daniel said, leaning on the counter, smiling over big teeth.

In my best Valley Girl, I mimicked, "My side is."

Dad's eyes grew large. "Get it done."

I pulled the full bag of garbage out of the plastic can. "Can we get some loot for tonight?"

Dad took out his wallet. "You need to get yourself a damn job."

"I have one. Chaperoning this clown." I nudged my chin at Daniel.

Dad spotted me a hundred-dollar bill. "Show the ladies a good time, huh?"

I held the cash up to a light that burned white over the sink. "Yep, real."

"Smartass," Dad said. "I want change."

My car's headlights beamed onto Adventureland's dirt parking lot. I parked toward the back.

Daniel closed his phone. "They're by the Ferris wheel."

I unbuckled my seatbelt and rubbed the back of my stiff neck. "Cool."

"It's go time," he said.

I stepped out of the car, insides twisting. Ride lights flashed. Roller coasters clanked. Pop music, chatter, and screams echoed. A breeze carried the smell of fried dough.

Daniel set the pace, weaving through the crowded park. My heart sped up to a dizzying pace.

Hailey sat alone on a bench, legs crossed. No sign of Lisa.

I felt pressure build behind my eyes. Unreal. Even Lisa was too good for me.

"Hi, guys," Hailey chirped, rising from the bench.

"Hey, Hailey," Daniel said.

She smiled, revealing white teeth behind moist, full lips. She had curves in all the right places.

Hailey shifted her blue eyes to me. "Lisa just ran to the bathroom."

I forced a smile.

"How was practice today?" she asked.

"Good," Daniel said. "Coach Fischer nearly lost it when some of the guys showed up late."

She giggled. "Sounds like a guy I wouldn't want to upset."

Daniel's voice dropped. "Yeah."

Uncomfortable silence.

Lisa Grant appeared out of the crowd, a red sweater hugging her thick body. Glitter sparkled on her smudged-pink eyelids. Shoulder-length dark hair fell flat across her face.

I rocked on the balls of my feet, my breaths leaking through clenched teeth.

Lisa smiled. "Hi, all."

I gulped. "Hey."

"Hey, girlfriend," Hailey said. "This is Andy. And Daniel. The Lembo brothers."

Lisa walked over to me, shook my hand. "Wow, Hailey usually sets me up with dogs. You, though. Very cute."

My face flushed.

Hailey backed into Daniel. "I didn't do so bad for myself."

Daniel hooked his arm around her waist.

"Not at all," Lisa said, dimples pressed in on her chubby cheeks.

We chatted for a few minutes, then I walked over to a ticket booth and purchased four ride bracelets.

Hailey snapped a plastic bracelet around her wrist. "Let's do Thunder Roller first."

"Which one's that?" I asked, hating the way my voice trailed off.

"That one." She pointed at the tallest coaster in the park. Naturally.

I folded my arms. "I'm not a big fan of heights. I'll watch you guys."

Lisa puffed her lower lip. "Aww. I'll hang back with you."

"No. Please, ride," I said.

She dropped her hand on my shoulder. "How 'bout we go on it just once? For me. I promise it won't be that bad."

I huffed. "Okay. Once."

She chewed her bottom lip. "What a sweetheart you are, Andy."

We got in the back of the Thunder Roller line and waited. I curled my fingers into and out of my pockets. It took about ten minutes before it was our turn. It felt more like an hour.

The coaster with orange and red flame decals rolled to a stop in front of us. The bars swung up and the riders stepped out. I hoped I wasn't going to black out. Or crap myself.

I stepped inside and sat. Lisa followed, making it a tight fit. The bar dropped. My hands squeezed the thick pads.

"Excited?" she asked.

"Oh, yeah," I said, my body stiff. "Can't you tell?"

The coaster kicked into gear. She laughed. "Life goes by fast. Sometimes you just have to let loose." She raised her meaty right arm straight up.

I looked at my white knuckles. "I'm just hoping to come out of this alive."

The coaster climbed. Slowly. Metal creaked beneath us.

Daniel, one car up, looked back at us. "Here we go. *Woot!*"

My heart thudding, I risked a glance down at the miniature cars dotting the lot.

The coaster crowned the track. I trapped my breath, gritted my teeth. We plunged, fast and hard. The bottom fell out of my stomach.

"Holy crap!" I yelled, as we zipped around the first curve.

More curves and drops. My head and arms vibrated like I was having a seizure. At long last, the brakes squealed. I peeled my hands from the bar.

Daniel helped Hailey up and out. I scooted out, wiped my palm dry and extended my hand to Lisa.

She took it and got up. "You're such a gentleman. Thanks."

I shrugged. "No prob."

Walking toward the exit, Hailey said, "That was awesome. Let's do it again."

I put up my hand. "I'm good."

"I'm good, too," Lisa said. "You two daredevils go ahead. We'll hang back and get to know each other."

"No kissing, you two." Hailey giggled and walked hand in hand with Daniel back to the end of the line.

Lisa twirled her hair around her index finger. "So, Andy … you play baseball, I hear."

"I try."

"I bet you're good."

"Nah. Not really."

She pulled a cell phone out of her purse. "Can I get your number?"

I gave it to her.

"Want mine?" she asked, her head tilted.

I patted my pockets. "Left my cell in my car. Actually, I should get it."

"I'll take a walk with you."

"Cool. Nice night." I looked toward the starlit sky.

"It's wonderful."

As we walked up the parking lot, we ran into Craig and Joey. Damn. Double damn. Daniel must have told them we were coming.

"What's up, cheeseball?" Craig asked.

I wanted to disappear. "Hey, guys."

Joey laughed. "No way. Is that Lembo?"

"Yep," I said.

"Where's Daniel and Hailey?" Craig asked, hands on hips.

"Thunder Roller."

Joey covered his mouth, coughed out laughs. "Wait, is this your chick?"

My cheeks flushed with rage, I looked at Lisa. Then I snapped my gaze back to Joey. "Shut up."

Joey stopped in front of Lisa and me. He spun his hat backward. "You guys do know there's a weight limit on these rides, right? Wouldn't want a cute couple like you getting hurt."

"Ease up," Craig said, a sharp edge to his features.

I felt like a coiled spring, ready to pop. "I don't mind you picking on me. But I do mind you picking on her."

Joey made a hissing sound. "Maybe she'll get hungry and eat that ugly goddamn scar off your face."

His words pounded into my chest. I made two tight fists.

Craig grabbed Joey's shoulder, yanked him backward. "C'mon, not cool. Leave 'em alone. Let's go find Daniel."

I glanced at Lisa. Tears wet her eyes. Rage engulfed me.

"Later," Joey said, walking away.

My temples pulsated. "Hey, asshole."

Joey and Craig turned around, their jaws hanging loose.

Joey's eyebrows drew together. "You better not be talking to me."

"What if I am?"

Joey broke for me.

I got low and locked up with him. Joey muscled me into a headlock then tossed me over his hip to the ground. Hard.

"Joey, what the fuck?" Craig hollered.

I tried to flip to my stomach, but Joey worked me until my shoulder blades were pinned to the dirt. He raised a closed fist.

I turned my head, scar side down. Shut my eyes.

Joey popped me, knuckles to cheekbone. Pain flooded my face.

Joey cocked his fist again. But the second punch didn't come. Craig clotheslined Joey, knocking him off me. Joey bounced up, grunted, and charged at Craig. They grappled, rolling on the ground.

A car's horn blew. Headlights pierced my vision.

Lisa lowered a hand, helped me up.

My hand over my eye, I staggered to the side of the road. The car passed by.

"What's wrong with you?" Craig asked, pacing. "He's my cousin."

Joey checked the scrapes on his forearm. "He's a prick."

"No. Maybe you're the prick. You need to get off the

'roids. Seriously, dude. You used to be cool to hang out with. Not anymore."

Joey flipped Craig the bird.

"Get the hell out of here," Craig said. "I'm not kidding. Just go."

Joey pointed at me. "You'll get yours."

"I don't think so," Craig said. "Touch him again and I'll tell Coach you've been juicing. Then you can kiss that wrestling scholarship goodbye."

"I'm not the one who changed. I'm outta here."

Joey marched to his yellow Lancer, backed the car up, peeled out and blew past us. A dust cloud lingered in the distance.

"You okay?" Craig asked.

I uncovered my throbbing face. "How's it look?"

"You'll survive," he said.

"Thanks, Andy," Lisa said, placing her hand on my shoulder. "Nobody's ever stood up for me like that."

"Like what? By getting my ass kicked?"

"Andy, I mean it. Thank you."

"I'm sorry he was such a jerk to you." I turned to Craig. "Is Joey really 'roiding?"

"Yeah. I actually injected him once. Dumbest thing I ever did. He's out of control with it now."

I licked the inside of my swollen cheek. "You using?"

"Nah. I like my nuts just like they are. Big."

I laughed despite the pain. "Thanks for saving my ass."

"Don't mention it. There's a first aid station by the bathrooms. Get some ice. You're gonna have a shiner."

I spat. "My face looks even more cryptic now, eh?"

Lisa smiled. "Aww. I think you're handsome. So very handsome."

"Come with me and get your eyes checked," I said.

We shared a laugh.

An icepack pressed to my face, I dialed Daniel on my cell. "Yo. Where you at?"

"Over by the games. Football toss."

"'Kay. You're not going to believe what just happened."

"What?"

"Hold on. We'll be there in a sec."

As we approached the game area, Daniel zipped footballs through holes in a backboard. Hailey cheered him on.

"You're a machine, Daniel," Craig called out.

Daniel spun around and stared at me. "Whoa. What happened to you?"

I pulled the pack off my face. "Joey Owens. That's what."

"No way. Shit."

I told him how it had gone down.

"Coach would kick him off the team if he knew he was using," Daniel said. "We can so get him kicked off."

Craig shook his head. "Don't. He'll take half the team with him."

I spit on the ground. "What do we do now? We know. If we don't tell and somebody finds out we knew, we could be in it deep."

"What proof you got?" Craig asked. "I was just joking about Joey juicing."

Right. I couldn't count on Craig bringing his pal down. "Guess we should keep the fight on the down low. Last thing we need is the team divided. Or Coach benching any of us."

Craig pulled out his cell. "Before Joey blabs about kicking your ass, I'll text him. Tell him to keep his fat trap shut. And we'll do the same. Right?"

"Right," I said.

Lisa smiled at me. "I think we should try this date night again some other time. Andy looks like he can use some aspirin and a soft pillow right about now."

Everyone agreed.

Daniel, Craig, and I walked the girls to Lisa's car. Daniel gave Hailey a hug. Then he kissed her cheek. Hailey put a finger to her lips. "I think you were looking for these."

Daniel laid one on her.

I opened the driver's-side door for Lisa and gave her a hug. "Get home safe."

"Thanks, Andy. You too."

She got in the car, clicked her seatbelt on. "Feel better."

"I will." I already did.

I pulled out of the Adventureland parking lot and merged onto Route 110.

"Joey texted me back," Craig said from the backseat. "He said to tell the punk that tonight never happened."

I put two hands on the wheel, blew out a breath. "So, how am I going to explain my face?"

"Tell everyone some drunk sucker-punched you," Daniel suggested.

"Makes me sound like a sissy. At least getting my ass kicked by Joey sounds cool."

Craig snaked forward, rested his forearms against the front seats. "You're lucky I was there. That's all I'm saying."

"I know…. I know."

Craig checked his look in the rearview mirror. "Let me smooth things over with Joey. He'll lay off you. Just don't give him a reason to kick your ass."

I switched lanes. "Deal."

After I dropped Craig off at his house, I drove a few hundred feet and pulled into our driveway.

"Some night," Daniel said, unbuckling his seatbelt.

"Yeah. Wild."

"You did a good thing, bro." He scratched at his head. "Wish I'd been there for you."

"Right. Joey would have twisted you into a pretzel."

Daniel laughed. "So, what'd ya think of Lisa?"

"She's okay. Not really any sparks, but you know. She's cool. I'll hang with her again. How 'bout Hailey?"

"Mad cool. I'm diggin' her."

"Figured," I said.

Daniel stuck out his fist. "So, we survived our first double date."

I touched my knuckles to his. "Barely."

CHAPTER 11

LIGHT FOG HUNG IN THE CHILLY AIR. A GROUNDSKEEPER swept a rake through a puddle behind the second-base bag while dark clouds gathered in the distance.

I put down my bat bag and wiped our team's bench dry with a towel. Coach walked up to me, tapping his clipboard on the side of his leg. "Your brother finally let loose on you?"

"Nah." A blush crept up my cheeks toward my forehead.

He winked. "I'm sure the other guy looks worse."

"Maybe." I hoped he'd drop the subject.

He did.

Craig spilled helmets out of a sack. He clapped, loud and obnoxious. "Let's go, boys. Play like champions today."

I scraped my fingernails on the ridges of the metal bench beneath me. My eyes followed the steady stream of players exiting the bus in the parking lot. The Huntington Blue Devils.

Their record was 3 and 3 for the year. Good enough for third place in our league.

Joey sat next to me. "You look like you got hit by a truck."

I matched his hard gaze. "Thanks."

"If you don't want to look worse, keep your lips shut 'bout whatever it is Craig told you. Understand?"

"Got it."

Joey stood up, twisted his mouth into a smile. "Cool."

Part of me wanted to tell Coach his superstar wrestler cheated. That the school's title was a fraud. That Joey should be kicked off for juicing. But the part of me that liked my body parts connected had a tad more say.

Daniel walked up to me, hat tipped up, his knuckles scrubbing his forehead. "You know what today is, right?"

"April nineteenth. Just another day."

His face swelled with bottled emotions. "Yeah."

I bent down, grabbed my glove out of my bat bag. "Wanna throw?"

"Sure," he said.

Daniel used to mail Mom a birthday card. He'd addressed it to our estranged grandparents—her parents—hoping for a reply, a thank you, anything. But those days were over. There was only so much disappointment a kid can handle. Daniel knew the cold, hard truth. Mom didn't care about us. She wasn't coming back. Not now. Not ever. But it still wasn't easy to deal with.

By game time, sunlight pierced through fast-moving gray clouds. Aunt Sue sat in the stands, a blanket over her lap. Dad and Uncle John balanced coffee cups while they climbed the mostly vacant bleachers. No sign of Hailey or Lisa. The smaller-than-usual crowd suited me just fine.

I walked out to the mound, my shin guards clanking. I dropped the ball into Craig's glove. "Ready?"

"Always," Craig said, a hard smile creasing his face. "I might throw a few wild ones. Ball's slippery as shit."

"I got you."

He glanced at the clouds then spat on the dirt. "Let's go. I wanna get this game in."

I jogged back behind the plate and lowered my mask.

The ump fiddled with his ball-strike clicker. "Batter up."

The leadoff batter, short and stocky, stuffed his oversized jersey into his baseball pants. "Let's go, Frankie. Be a hitter up there," the third base coach called out. Frankie choked up on the bat, settled into a stance.

Craig narrowed his eyes at me, his glove perched in front of his chest. I flashed signs between my legs. Outside fastball.

Craig nodded then wound up. His pitch hummed into my mitt. Strike one.

Frankie watched two outside pitches go by then put the sweet spot of his bat to the ball, driving a hard shot to right field. Daniel charged in, stuck his mitt out and made a terrific shoestring catch. One out.

"Nice play," I called out, mask up.

"Nice face," the next hitter, thin and tall, said.

I pretended not to hear him and moved my target inside. Hoping Craig would plunk this jerk.

"Let's go, Tyler! Let's go, Tyler!" a player chanted from the Huntington bench.

Pansy name.

Craig wound up and threw a lifeless pitch. Tyler ripped the ball into the left centerfield gap.

Jerome slipped on his way to retrieve the ball. Fell butt-flat on the grass. The ball rolled to the fence. Pete tracked it down. He crow-hopped, then overthrew the cutoff man.

In foul territory, Tommy lumbered to Pete's errant throw. A complete circus out there.

I readied myself for a play at the plate.

But no throw came. Tyler blurred by me. Got mobbed by his teammates: 1-0.

Craig paced the mound, muttering to himself. "Shake it off," I said, walking toward him, straightening my chest protector.

He waved me back. "I'm fine. We'll get the next guy."

Craig regrouped and got the next two batters. Both groundouts to Mike at short. Inning over.

Behind the backstop, I peeled off catcher's gear and popped on a batting helmet.

"Start us off," Daniel said, holding up a clenched fist.

"Awesome play on that one," I said.

"Thanks. Didn't know if I should let it bounce."

"You chose wisely." I grabbed two bats off the rack.

"This guy can throw." Daniel was looking out at the pitcher.

"Larson's their ace," I said. It seemed like teams were deliberately arranging their rotation to throw their best at us.

I took practice cuts with both bats, timing Larson's practice pitches. As I returned a bat to the rack, my chest tightened. Likely a gas bubble. But my thoughts clicked to my heart. To Dad's brother. Now my breathing felt labored, forced. The ground felt rubbery beneath me as I walked out to the field. Why is this happening?

My teammates cheered me on.

I told myself I was fine, that it was all in my head. But my body didn't listen. I tensed to the point of pain, my neck and shoulders taking the brunt.

Coach flashed me the take sign. Good. I could stand at the plate. I thought. I plowed my right cleat through crusted mud and lifted my gaze to the pitcher.

Larson wiped his chin on his left shoulder. Standing about six feet, he looked more linebacker than pitcher.

I got in a low stance, twirled the bat. Larson wound up, dealt a fastball high and wide.

I stepped out of the box and quietly burped. *It's just gas. Relax, Andy.*

My gaze swept across the field. I took it all in. The sunlit, moist grass. The players. The way my hands felt around the bat handle. The smells of baseball. The sound of my name being chanted. The game was doing what no drug ever could. Calming me.

I took a practice swing and reentered the batter's box. I could do this.

I watched Larson's next pitch go by, an inside strike.

I drew in a deep breath, slowly exhaled. It was go time.

Larson kicked up his leg and hurled a letter-high fastball. I chopped down at it. Bounced the ball to the shortstop. I tore down the baseline, expecting to hear the ball pop into the first base baseman's glove. The throw never came. The shortstop botched the play.

"My bad," the shortstop said, lobbing the ball to the pitcher.

I jogged back to the bag, my baseball juices flowing.

Pete adjusted the straps on his batting gloves and eyed Coach, who gave us the hit-and-run sign.

I established my lead, my fingers dancing at my sides.

When Larson lifted his left leg, I got a good jump.

Pete slapped a grounder down the first base line. I chugged along, teeth grinding, fists pumping.

Coach waved me to third and kept his arm whirling. "Go! Go! Go!"

I rounded third, floored it home. The catcher reeled in a bouncing throw. I hook-slid around him, my hand licking the plate.

"Safe," the ump called, his arms axing air.

Sucking wind, I bounced up and brushed dirt off my pants. My teammates crowded me. Shook my helmet. Gave me fives.

Nathan patted my back. "Yeah, Andy. That's what I'm talkin' about."

Joey stuck out an open palm. "Way to hustle."

I slapped his hand. "Thanks."

Maybe Joey's changed, I thought. *Maybe things'll be different between us.*

Maybe. But I doubted it.

The game had been close up until the fourth inning. That's when our bats caught fire. Six Panthers crossed home plate. Plenty of breathing room for Craig, up 10-3. Hailey and Lisa arrived in the bottom of the sixth. They sat in the front row of the bleachers, puffy jackets zipped to their necks. Clipping on my shin guards, I smiled at them. They waved at me, giggling.

I turned my head just in time to see Kevin bounce into an inning-ending double play.

I picked my mask off the ground and jogged to my position.

"Woot! Woot! Go, Andy," Lisa called out.

I could feel my face flush and felt sweat collecting on the back of my neck.

After I caught Craig's warm-up pitches, he motioned me to the mound. I stood up, lifted my mask, and glanced at the ump. He was over by the Blue Devils dugout, refilling his water bottle.

"Hey, catcher," Tyler said, standing just outside the batter's box, a bat tucked under his arm.

"What?" I asked, my tone clipped.

A frown of concentration heavy on his features, he said, "Do us all a favor and keep that mask on."

Anger seethed behind my hard stare. Yeah, I wanted to clock him. But I knew I'd just be taking the bait. Tyler wanted me to snap. To start a brawl.

My lips pinched tight and nostrils flaring, I turned my back to him and headed out to the mound. My pride taking a beating.

"What'da fuck he say?" Craig asked, rubbing down the ball.

"Forget him. Just close the game out."

Craig removed his cap, wiped sweat from his forehead. "He say something about your face?"

I tapped my mitt on Craig's chest. "I need you to stay focused. Three outs. That's what I need from you."

"I'm *so* gonna peg that string bean."

I looked away, then back at Craig. "He's not worth it. He'll charge. We'll brawl. Players'll get suspended. It won't matter to them. To us, it will. Like you said, let's play like champions. Now strike this asshole out."

He spat. "Whatever. Let's go."

I returned to my position and squatted. Held my mitt motionless over the middle of the plate.

Tyler strangled the bat handle, cocked his elbow.

Craig kicked up his leg and hurled a pitch that rode in on Tyler's knees.

Tyler danced out of the way.

Damn, Craig could be a thickheaded idiot.

Tyler gave Craig an evil stare then reentered the batter's box.

In the crouch, I flashed signs between my legs. Curveball.

Tyler, in his stance, glanced back at me. "Better not throw at me again."

Dick.

Craig hung his curveball over the middle of the plate. Tyler roped the ball to third base. Tommy stuck out his glove and snagged it in flight. One down.

Tyler beat his bat into the dirt. Flung his helmet.

"There's no place for that garbage here, coach," the ump said. "I'll throw the next player out. You have your warning."

Craig got the next batter to ground out to second.

Down to their final out, the Huntington Blue Devils went to their bench and sent in a lanky kid. Behind in the count, the batter popped it up in front of home plate. I threw my mask off and circled under the ball. Squeezed it. Game over.

Cheers echoed from the crowd.

I gave Craig a high five. "Way to pitch."

"You played good, kid."

I grinned; he was right. Three hits. A stolen base. Threw out two base stealers.

Daniel jogged over to us. "Great game, guys."

"Go ahead," Craig said to me. "Do your gay handshake with your brother."

I made my shoulders dance. "Join us. You know you wanna."

Craig cringed, but ended up taking part. A three-way shake and bump.

CHAPTER 12

"**Y**OU BRINGIN' YOUR GLOVE?" DANIEL ASKED, HIS chest bare, a Mets T-shirt dangling from his hand.

I opened my dresser drawer. "Duh. Craig said the seats are sick. Right behind the Mets' dugout."

"We'll feel the breeze off Chris Pyron's pitches."

"You mean the breeze off the Padres' whiffs." I gripped a pair of rolled-up tube socks, turned and fired it at his six-pack abs.

"You wanna feel a breeze?" He squatted, made a face, and squeezed out a juicy fart.

I pinched my nose. "Jeez. What did you eat?"

He shrugged, hands turned up. "C'mon. Department stores could bottle this smell and make a killing."

"You got the *kill* part right."

Dressed, we met up with Dad in the kitchen.

Dad worked a knife through an orange. "We'll take the train to the stadium. John's going to meet us there."

I huffed.

Dad glanced at me then stared down at his orange.

Train rides gave me anxiety. Dad knew this. My last train ride, a few years ago, nearly sent me into a full-scale panic attack. Not that Dad cared then. Or now.

Daniel swung open the fridge door. "What time we leaving?"

Dad coughed into his fist. "After breakfast. Let's make batting practice."

Dad steered his old-new Malibu into a parking spot at the Central Islip train station. A Sunday morning, there were plenty of spots open. I grabbed my glove and baseball off the floor mat then stepped out of the car. My breath hurried, I told myself not to think about the train ride. But being here, seeing the tracks, I couldn't ignore it.

Daniel tugged up his jeans then stuck out his open mitt. "Toss it here."

I flipped him the baseball.

He leaned against Dad's car, ankles crossed, studying the ball. "I hope somebody good signs it."

I curled my lips over my teeth. "Nah, I don't want to sign my own stuff."

He laughed and handed me the ball back.

As we climbed the train platform steps, my limbs tingled. My insides clenched.

Dad shoved his hands into the pockets of his Mets sweatshirt. "I'll get the tickets. It's cheaper to buy before you board." He flanked left to the ticket office. Daniel and I walked up the platform, bars of sunlight shining down, our shadows stretching tall before us.

Up ahead on the platform, a boy, sixish, punched his fist into a child-sized mitt. He walked behind an elderly woman pushing a stroller. I thought of my Grandma Betty and the lone baseball game she'd come to watch. Daniel played up a year, but the rest of us on the team were twelve. Grandma Betty had put her high-pitched voice to work when she called Daniel and me over to sit on her lap. Our teammates had a field day with that one.

Train-crossing lights flashed. A bell rang. The long bar lowered. Vehicles slowed to a halt.

I threw a glance behind me, my stomach knotted. Train headlights appeared in the distance. As I turned my head back around, my eyes snapped to the boy. He held his arms out like airplane wings, his walking pattern veering him close to the edge of the platform.

The elderly woman twisted around, her eyes bulging behind bottle-thick glasses. "Johnny, get away from —"

Johnny's ankle rolled. He plunged to the tracks like a brick, a five-foot drop.

I let my glove and ball fall to the pavement, the boy's scream ripping through me. The lady shrieked, her hands flying to her face.

I sprinted toward the boy, throwing glances over my shoulder at the train.

Daniel rode my tail. "Train's going through!"

The train's whistle blew, long and loud. Metal brakes grinded. Sparks flew.

I stopped at the edge of the platform, squatted, reached down to the boy. "Grab my hands!"

The boy staggered toward me, crying, hands extended.

Daniel leaped by me, onto the tracks. He got behind the boy, scooped him up by his armpits. The platform rumbled, the face of the train screaming toward us.

I locked hold of the boy's arms and hoisted him up. The boy and I crashed to the platform pavement.

The train whooshed by.

Lying face down on the cement, I squeezed my eyes shut.

"Johnny," the old woman's voice cried. "Grandma's here. You're okay, Johnny. Thank God, you're okay."

I steeled myself, then lifted my head and looked to my right. No sign of Daniel.

No, God . . . I swiveled my head to the left.

On the platform, down on a knee, Daniel gave me the thumbs-up sign. My gaze met his. He winked.

I hopped to my feet. The boy, hysterical, ran into his grandmother's open arms.

Daniel stood. "You all right, kid?" Daniel said.

The boy continued to sob, offering no reply.

Daniel walked over to me, nodding. I clapped the hump of his shoulder. "Whoa. I thought I lost you, bro."

Rubbing at the back of his neck, Daniel said, "My life flash before my eyes. Can't believe what just happened."

I looked out at the train, now stopped on the tracks a couple hundred yards beyond the platform. "What you did ... holy shit. You have freaking balls of steel!"

He pointed at me. "What *we* did."

Dad jogged up to us, our baseball gloves stacked in his left hand. After coughing hard, he said, "Tell me I didn't see what I thought I saw. Are you nuts? I mean it. Are you insane?"

Daniel smiled. Dad stood tall, his face glowing. "You're a damn hero. That's what you are. A damn hero."

Daniel looked at me. "Andy, too."

Dad's smile died. He put his hands on hips, moved his eyes over me. "C'mon now. Sticking out a hand to help is one thing. Jumping in front of a train is another."

Screw you.

Guilt and anger erupted within me. Why didn't I jump down? What was wrong with me? The boy would have died if Daniel hadn't done what he did. I would have let him die.

The old woman pushed her baby stroller over to us, Johnny latched to her thigh. Tears trickled down her wrinkled face. "You boys saved my grandson. I should've been paying more attention. I'm so sorry. So sorry. Thank you, young men. Thank you."

She addressed us both, but I knew which one of us she meant. Her eyes stayed on Daniel. When her gaze drifted my way, she gave me a what-happened-to-your-face look.

"You're welcome," Daniel said, touching his fingers to the woman's arm. "Is he okay?"

"Johnny's fine. Are you young fellows okay?"

"We're fine."

A heavyset railroad worker exited the train station and jogged over to us, his keys jingling, a walkie-talkie in his hands.

"Everyone okay? A conductor said he saw people on the tracks."

"Yes, nobody hurt," Daniel said.

The old woman went on to tell the worker what had happened. The worker radioed the conductor and said that all was good and that it was okay to proceed west, meaning it was that close. The conductor didn't even know.

The train pulled away, fading into the distance. I walked over to the spot where the kid lost his balance. Looking down at the tracks, I dug my fingernails into my palm. Seconds separated life from death. Seconds.

It didn't take long for my mind to loop a different outcome. Daniel not getting to the boy in time, their blood staining the silver rails, limbs scattered in the brush.

I squeezed my eyes shut, colored dots floating in the darkness. The full scope of what had happened was hitting me. Hard.

I slowly reopened my eyes. *We saved a life. We saved a family the grief of burying a child.*

I wanted to believe that the little boy was safe now. That he'd get to grow old. But I knew there were no guarantees. There were no safe places for a child. Not on a train platform. Not inside a car. Not inside a school. Not inside a home.

Danger was everywhere.

I touched my fingertips to my scar.

A heartbeat away from death. All of us.

I walked over to Daniel, knocked his arm with the back of my hand. "Way to go, dude. You really came through."

He smiled, blinking his eyes as a gust of wind blew.

The platform shook. A Manhattan-bound train rolled up to the station.

"This is us," Dad said.

"What are your names, boys?" the old woman asked. "I want to light a candle for you."

"Andy and Daniel Lembo," Daniel said.

"Thank you. From the bottom of my heart. Thank you. May God bless you."

The train doors opened. Passengers stepped out.

"Take care," Daniel said, waving as he followed Dad into the train.

I stepped on board, my head heavy with emotions. Scared to ride in a train. And then there was Daniel, fearlessly jumping in front of one. *I'm such a pansy. What's wrong with me?*

I sat next to Daniel. Dad handed us each a ticket, then sat in a seat a few rows up from us.

"I'm sorry," I said, hugging myself.

"For what?"

"I should've been the one to go down. I got there first. I'm the big brother."

Daniel elbowed me. "You tried what you thought would

work. You went to help him. That's what counts."

"Bullshit. The kid would've gotten hit. He would've died."

"You don't know that."

I took off my baseball hat, messed with my hair. "I can't believe you jumped down there. Like something out of a freaking movie."

He bit on his lower lip. "If the baseball thing doesn't work out for me, maybe I've got a career as a stuntman."

I laughed. "Or a superhero. Super-Dan."

He leaned back in his seat and smiled. "Super-Dan. I like that."

We switched to another train at the Woodside stop. Daniel's leap and rescue kept replaying in my thoughts. So much so, I almost forgot how much I hated being in trains. Almost.

"This is our stop," Dad said. "Citi Field."

I followed Daniel and him off the train. The ballpark loomed in the distance. We joined the flow of the crowd. Hot dogs sizzled on grills. Vendors hawked Mets scorebooks, other baseball paraphernalia. The closer we got to the stadium, the more my negative emotions gave way to pure excitement.

Dad handed us each a Mets ticket and we entered the stadium through a turnstile.

Dad looked down at his ticket stub. "This way."

We rode the escalator up one flight. Dad led us to our field-level section. Prior to that day, upper-deck seating was as close as I'd gotten to a Major League field.

I walked through a double doorway and gaped as I took in a magnificent view: the Mets players warming up on the picture-perfect baseball field.

A gray-haired usher showed us to our seats, ten rows back from the Mets dugout. Dad slapped a few bucks in the man's hand.

"Enjoy the game," the usher said.

"We will," Dad said.

"Wright's taking BP." Daniel's eyes were wide and bright.

"Nice," I said. David Wright was Daniel's favorite player, his idol. Had been since he was called up from Norfolk.

Daniel took out his digital camera and snapped a few shots.

"Let's go down," I said, pointing at fans standing in the front row by the railing.

Daniel and I walked down the steps and found a spot in front to stand and watch from. David Wright launched a moonshot over the left field wall that needed a billboard to take it down.

I shook Daniel's shoulder.

Daniel bumped me. "Holy crap. See how that thing sailed?"

David Wright pulled off his helmet and strolled behind the batting cage. A smile ratcheted up on his face as he chatted with a teammate.

Juan Salata batted next. He bunted the first two pitches before taking hacks.

Daniel elbowed my arm. "This is so cool. I'll be right back. Nature's calling."

"'Kay."

He scampered up the stadium steps.

David Wright walked toward the dugout. I was so excited I could hardly breathe. I could see the scruff on his face!

"Way to hit, Wright," some kid my age called out.

Other fans chanted his name.

Wright flashed a thousand-watt smile.

"David, can you sign this?" A girl with golden blonde hair, twelvish, held a pen and piece of paper out over the wall.

But Wright had disappeared into the dugout.

Salata took swings, batted the ball around the field. Wright emerged from the dugout, his fielder's glove tucked under his arm. Fans called out his name. He walked over to the crowd. "Who's got something for me to sign?"

More fans rushed over, packing in tight. I felt closed in, lightheaded.

After signing for a few fans, he said, "Enjoy the game, guys. I gotta go."

It was now or never. "David! Just one more," I leaned over the railing, holding out my ball and pen.

His eyes locked on mine. Or maybe it was my scar. "Sure."

I handed him my ball and pen, my hand trembling, and he signed the ball.

"Thank you," I squeaked.

"No prob," he said. Then he jogged out to the field.

The ball electric in my hands, I returned to my seat. "Check it out." I handed Dad the baseball. "David Wright."

"Sure is. Might be worth good money someday," Dad said, glancing at it before handing it back.

"Yeah," I said, my jaw clenched.

I expected him to show a shred of excitement. Something. Anything. But he didn't need to tell me where his mind was. He was ashamed of me. Ashamed I let Daniel jump down and help the boy. Ashamed I didn't do it myself. I risked Dad's grand plan to be the father of a famous pitcher. I risked Dad's future, his everything.

Daniel returned, his eyes glued to the action on the field while he returned to his seat. I poked his shoulder with the ball. He grabbed it from me. "No way. I missed him signing?"

"You snooze, you lose."

"Oh man, what did he say?" Daniel peered at the ball from different angles.

"Not much. Our thumbs touched."

"Shut up. So cool."

Dad stood up. "I'm gonna get a soda. Want anything?"

"I'll take a hotdog and a Coke," Daniel said.

"I'm good," I said, not caring if Dad heard the edge in my voice.

Dad shuffled to the aisle and walked up the steps. I looked out at the players shagging fly balls.

"Look at the way he signs." Daniel cupped the ball in his hands like he was holding crystal.

"It's yours. Happy birthday."

He made a face. "Right. Nice try."

"Seriously. I know you have a crush on the guy."

He chuckled. "Dude, it's your ball."

My eyes met his. "I'll trade you. Get me a teamed-signed something when you make the pros."

His face lit up. "You're serious, aren't you? I can have this?"

I nodded.

"No backsies?"

I put my glove down on my seat. "No backsies. Just don't tell Dad."

"Why?"

"Just don't."

"Deal. Thanks, bro." His dimples were shining hard.

The Mets were already down 4-0 by the time Uncle John arrived in the top of the third inning. "Sorry I'm late," he said, easing his large body into a seat between Dad and Daniel. "They're getting spanked, eh?"

Daniel leaned forward in his seat, arms folded. "The Padres went yard twice already."

Uncle John scratched stubble under his chin. "Pyron's usually money. So, how do you like the seats?"

"Great," Dad said. "Danny Boy almost didn't make it here. Go ahead, tell him what you did."

Daniel's face flushed. "It was nothing. I helped a kid off the railroad tracks."

Dad clapped his knees, wheezed. "Nothing? Learn how to tell a story, son. Stop being so damn modest."

Daniel shrugged.

Dad went on to boast to Uncle John about what Daniel did. All Daniel. As if I did nothing.

"Well, all right," Uncle John said, nodding at Daniel. "Sounds like I'm sitting next to a hero. They should print you up in the papers."

"Andy pulled the kid up from the tracks," Daniel added. "I couldn't have done it without him."

Uncle John looked over at me. "Not many people can say they saved a life. You guys did a great thing. You should be proud."

"Can I get you a beer?" Dad asked.

Uncle John pulled out his wallet. "My treat today. What do you guys want?"

I stood and clapped, my ears awash in the roar of the crowd.

The Mets had won. Wright hit a walk-off homer and the stadium rocked with 42,000 fans shaking the stadium while Dad, Daniel, Uncle John, and I exchanged high fives.

Daniel pumped his fist. "How friggin' awesome," he said.

Wright paraded around the bases. Got trounced by his teammates at home plate.

I clapped in rhythm with the crowd. "Can't ask for a better game than that," I said.

An AC/DC song blared on the stadium's sound system and Daniel played air guitar. "What a day," he said.

"Amazing," I said. "Damn, I love this game."

CHAPTER 13

WHILE MRS. HEARST DRONED ON ABOUT THE CIVIL War, I spread my hands on my desk, eager for the school day to end. Acid swirled in my stomach. My gaze drifted out the window. A muggy day. Gray clouds. The forecast called for rain. Lots of it.

I flipped to the back page of my notebook, where I tracked baseball stats. We were atop our league, 14 and 1. Grovetown, at 12 and 2, was nipping our heels. In our first meeting, they beat us. But Daniel wasn't pitching that game. Today things would be different, if the rain held off.

I calculated my batting average. Year-to-date: .354. *Finally back over the .350 threshold.*

The bell jolted me out of my daze. I found my feet and exited the classroom.

I met up with Daniel at his hallway locker. "Looks like crap out there," I said.

"Did it start raining?" He touched his fingers to his flipped-up hair.

"Not yet. It's dark though." I shoved my hand in my pocket. "What class you got?"

"Trig."

I smirked. "Sucks for you."

He closed his locker. "Must be nice to be a senior."

Hailey and Lisa approached us. "Hey, boys," Hailey said. She was chewing gum and her books were tucked under her arm.

"Hey," Daniel said.

Lisa smiled at me. "Ready for your big game?" she asked.

"If by 'ready' you mean is my stomach upset, then yes, I'm ready."

Hailey tossed her blond hair from one shoulder to the other. "Aww, you'll do great," she said. "We'll be cheering you guys."

"Bring your umbrellas," Daniel said.

Hailey snuggled up to Daniel. "Know what today is?"

He shrugged. "Thursday?"

"No, silly. Our one-month anniversary."

He chuckled. "Sorry, cutie. Forgot that one." He gave her a peck on the lips.

Lisa and I rolled our eyes. Lisa and I were good friends. So far, that was the extent of it.

We chatted a bit more then went our separate ways.

I had some time before the game, so I stopped at my hall locker and gave it an overdue cleaning. Got rid of sandwich bags, scrap paper, and such.

While I strode down the gleaming hallway, my focus shifted to my breathing. A knot twisted in my stomach. My mouth filled with bile. I swallowed it back down.

Fucking anxiety.

I quickened my pace, hiccupping dry heaves. A dull pain throbbed behind my temples. I rounded the corner and detoured into the bathroom, sending the door crashing into the wall. A kid no bigger than me followed my reflection. I entered the bathroom stall, lips quivering. *Don't throw up*, I told myself. *Relax, Andy.*

I sat on the bowl and covered my eyes with my hands. *Breathe in, breathe out. Breathe in, breathe out.*

Somebody wearing huge black sneakers entered the bathroom. I dropped my pants. He entered the stall next to mine.

I sat and waited. Once the bathroom cleared out, I stood and pulled up my pants. Staring into the bowl, I felt a gag swelling up. Then I flipped up the lid and puked. I slid my palm up my forehead and pushed up my bangs, embarrassed. Damn, why was my anxiety so hard to control?

I opened the stall door and moped over to a sink. I kept my eyes on the running faucet, anything to avoid seeing my ugly mug in the mirror. I dried with paper towels and exited.

The ground shaky beneath me, I walked down the hallway. I entered the locker room, urging myself to think positive. Pulling open the door to the varsity section, I looked at Tommy, Pete, and Joey—the early birds.

"What's up, Andy?" Pete asked from where he sat on a bench. He kicked off his sneaker.

"Not too much," I said.

Joey took off his shirt, flexed. "Yo, Andy, isn't Grovetown the team you choked against?"

No, it's the game I replaced you as the starter in. "Thanks for the reminder."

"No prob." Joey stepped onto the scale.

"We all sucked that game," Pete said. "Can't play like that again if we expect to win today."

I lined up batting helmets on the ground behind the backstop. Swollen rainclouds cast shadows over the prepped baseball field.

Daniel swaggered over to me, his glove hanging from his hand. "Wanna throw?"

"Yeah." I picked a baseball out of a bucket of balls.

"Here they come." He nudged his chin toward the Grovetown players. They were out by the parking lot, making their way down the path to the field.

We jogged out by third base and soft tossed. Tension sloughed off my body, the sights and sounds of the game doing their job.

He sailed a throw over my head. The ball rolled to a metal wastebasket in foul territory. A crow, perched on the wastebasket's rim, took flight. As I ran toward the ball, my cleat caught on something. I fell, face first. Hard.

Laughter echoed around me. I lifted my head, more embarrassed than hurt.

"That was too damn funny," Joey yelled from the outfield. "Where's a video camera when you need one?"

"You okay?" Daniel jogged up to me.

I got up. "I'm fine."

Some of the Grovetown players chuckled as they passed me.

"What happened?" Daniel asked.

"Duh, I tripped on something."

"I see it…." He pulled a tent stake out from the ground.

"What the hell's that doing here?" I asked.

"Only you, Andy. Only you'd trip on something like this on a baseball field."

"You're right. Only me. My arm's warmed up. You?"

"Yeah, I'm good."

After we took fielding practice, Coach called the team in. We gathered by our bench. He stood in his usual wood-statue stance and spat sunflower seeds. "I don't need to tell you guys the importance of today's game. First place is on the line. Grovetown wants it. You see them strutting around over there. They think they're hot shit. The better team. Prove them wrong. Play tough. Play smart. Most of all, play with heart. Leave no doubt. Let's go, Panthers. All hands in."

We piled hands.

I spied Dad, Uncle John, Aunt Sue, Lisa, and Hailey among those packed onto the bleachers. Our school had been pumping this game all week, announcing it during the morning announcements and such. *Newsday*, Long Island's biggest newspaper, had run a feature about today's matchup in their high school sports section. Daniel, of course, was the focus. But I got to see my name in print, too, a brief mention about me being Daniel's catcher and brother.

Scouts and press readied their equipment behind the backstop. I suited up in catcher's gear and took my position. Daniel ratcheted down the heat on his warm-up pitches, throwing mostly junk. I caught his final warm-up pitch, stood, and whipped the ball down to Kevin at second base.

Daniel motioned me to the mound. I hustled out.

He rubbed down the ball. "Ready to do this?"

"As I'll ever be. Place is swarming with scouts."

"Let's give 'em a show."

I nodded. "Watch the leadoff batter. He started last game off with a bunt."

"Yeah. A fast little shit. Give me an outside target. I wanna see if he squares."

"'Kay." I stuck out my knuckles. "Let's go, bro."

He tapped my knuckles with his. "It's show time."

Derrick Sardi choked up on the bat, got into a low stance. I crouched down, my heart thudding against my chest protector.

I flashed Daniel the fastball sign and shifted my target to the outer half of the plate.

Daniel wound up, snarled. Sardi squared, bunted. The ball rolled out in front of the plate.

I sprang to my feet, ripping off my mask, swept up the ball, turned and fired to first. A bang-bang play. The ump punched air. One out.

"Yeah!" Daniel yelled, pumping his fist.

The crowd cheered. My body tingled. I pointed at Daniel.

"Way to throw it," Coach called. "Nice play."

Daniel had no trouble with the next two batters, striking them out with a steady stream of gas. I traded catcher's gear for a batting helmet. Staring at the barrel of my black bat, my thoughts shifted to my last at bat against this team.

When the bat slipped out of my hands.

When I watched strike three go by and cost my team the game.

"Start us up," Daniel said, slapping me five.

I threw a glance at the crowd. Lisa waved at me, giggling. I nodded at her then tentatively stepped out to the field.

Coach signaled me to take a pitch. No surprise. My teammates were up, cheering.

Eric Herman, standing at the cusp of the mound, lifted his cap and ran his hand through his hair. I imagined Hailey and Lisa giddy over his dreamy good looks.

I got into a low stance and waved my bat.

Herman stood on the pitching rubber, his glove curled on his hip.

A surge of adrenaline cut my breath short.

The pitcher wound up, hurled a fastball that I watched go by. Strike one.

I swung over the next pitch, a nasty curveball.

In the hole, 0 and 2, I choked up the bat, determined not to go down looking.

Eric snapped a curveball. I flinched, tucking the bat into myself. The ball broke back over the plate. Strike three.

"Shit," I whispered, my head down. I had to give credit to Herman, though. His pitches were spot-on. The kid was good. Damn good.

"Get 'em next time," Pete said, slapping me another five as I passed.

Herman took care of Pete and Jake as well, getting them to ground out. A quick 1-2-3 inning.

Both pitchers continued to mow down hitters through the first three innings, no hits allowed. In the fourth inning, Pete singled, breaking up Herman's no-hit game attempt. Jake followed with a base hit of his own. But Tommy's whiff ended the threat. Another scoreless inning.

Daniel got sharper as the innings cranked on. It just didn't seem fair. His pitches had it all. Accuracy. Speed. Movement.

Nobody on our team spoke the words "no-hitter," it being a jinx and all. But both teams, most everyone watching, knew what was going on. Daniel was three outs from history. With the score knotted at zero, Daniel was also a pitch away from being on the losing end of this game. And then there was the chance the rainclouds would burst open.

"Bottom of the sixth," Nathan called out, tapping his index finger on the scorebook. "Daniel leads off. Then the top of the order. Let's go."

I pulled on a batting glove. "Help your cause."

Daniel popped on a helmet. "We just need one run. Just one."

"Do it," I said.

He walked up to the plate and got into his stance.

"Here we go, Daniel! Let's go, Daniel!" I cheered from the on-deck circle.

Herman wound up, hung a curveball. Daniel sat back on the pitch and roped the ball down the third-base line. The third baseman dove, but couldn't smother it.

"Go! Go!" I screamed.

Daniel rounded first base and coasted into second base. I picked up his bat from the grass and tossed it to Pete.

Daniel, standing on the second base bag, pointed at me.

I nodded.

Coach flashed me dummy signs. I stepped in the batter's box, waved my bat.

Eric's first pitch broke into the dirt. The catcher lunged to block it, but it scooted by him. Daniel advanced ninety feet.

I took a deep breath, expecting Herman's next pitch to be a fastball. And that's what came. I turned on the pitch and lifted the ball to left field. I sprinted down the baseline.

The left fielder drifted in and caught it.

Daniel tagged up, running hard, his head down.

The cutoff throw came in offline and bounced into foul territory. He scored.

I met up with him behind the backstop. He spun his helmet on the ground saying, "Yeah, bro. That was clutch."

I slapped him five. "There's your cushion. Let's do this."

After Daniel finished his warm-up pitches, I jogged out to the mound. "Three outs, kid," I said. I tapped my mitt on his chest. "That's what I need from you."

He nodded. "I got it."

I tapped him once more. "The meat of their order's coming up. Let's go. Bring it."

I jogged back to my position, lowered my mask, squatted, and flashed a sign. Fastball.

Daniel nodded and rocked his body into motion.

The batter got a piece of Daniel's low pitch, dinking a grounder to Mike at short. He vacuumed it up and fired to first. One down.

Two outs away from the record books.

Mattelson stepped up to the plate, his massive hands strangling the bat handle. He had been the only Grovetown player to get good hacks in versus Daniel. He was 0 for 2, but both outs came on hard-hit balls.

I pushed out a breath and gave Daniel the fastball sign. He nodded.

I clenched my fist behind my back, fingernails digging into my palm. He wound up, threw a fastball into Gary's wheelhouse. Gary put his bat's metal barrel to the ball, blasting a long, high drive down the left-field line. If it was fair, it was gone.

"Foul ball," the field ump called, his arm axing down. Whew.

The home plate ump threw Daniel a new ball. I called for time and scampered out to the mound.

"That was close," Daniel said, his eyes wide.

"Seriously."

"Now's a good time to throw a deuce. He's guessing fastball."

"No way. Come back with the heat. You can blow it by this guy."

Daniel bent his hat brim. "It's your call, bro."

"The heat," I said.

A sharp clap of thunder rumbled in the distance.

"C'mon. Let's get this game in, bro," I said, knocking knuckles with him.

I snapped my mask on and returned to my position. He stared in at me, his glove poised in front of his chest.

I gave him the fastball sign. He wound up, smooth and poetic.

Swinging with force, Gary belted the ball.

A comebacker.

The whistling line drive nailed Daniel in the head.

Daniel staggered.

Collapsed.

He lay face down on the mound, his glove tucked under his chest.

Gasps and screams echoed as I stood, my body going cold. "Daniel!"

Kenneth Finn, our team's trainer, sprinted out to him. I ran over next, tossing my mask to the ground.

Kenneth felt his neck, checked for a pulse. "Daniel, can you hear me? Nod if you can hear me."

"Daniel, goddammit, nod," I said, my hand flat on his back. I turned to Kenneth. "What's happening? Why isn't he moving?"

Kenneth didn't answer me.

He put smelling salt to Daniel's nose while players, coaches, and fans gathered around.

The umps suspended the game. Mattelson kept repeating how sorry he was. Press camera people snapped shots.

Our school's nurse kneeled next to Daniel. "I called 911. What can I do to help?"

Kenneth stood up. "He's got a pulse, but he's out cold. Let's get him a blanket."

Coach brought over a blanket. Kenneth draped it over him. I slugged over to my family. Pressure built behind my eyes.

Dad paced beside the mound, his eyes wide open like a bug, his hands locked behind his head. Hailey, hysterical, hugged Lisa.

Uncle John, Nathan and Craig stood frozen, somber expressions on their faces.

Aunt Sue rubbed my back. "He'll be okay, Andy. I promise."

I blinked my eyes fast and hard. A lump lodged in my throat. "He's not waking up. Why isn't …" My body heated up and teary floodgates opened down my ruined face.

Sirens wailed. Lights flashed in the parking lot. An ambulance and a police SUV stormed down the pebbled path, onto the baseball field.

"Back up, folks," Kenneth said. "Give them space."

Two male EMTs worked a stretcher out of the back of the ambulance. A burly female EMT with salt-and-pepper hair rushed over to Daniel. She knelt down and took his pulse. "What's his name?"

"Daniel," Kenneth said.

"Daniel, talk to me," the EMT said. "Come back to us, Daniel. What happened to him?"

"A baseball struck him in the head," Kenneth told her.

They rolled the stretcher up to Daniel. Placed an oxygen mask on him. Keeping him in the same position he'd fallen in, they lifted him onto a backboard, and then strapped him onto the stretcher.

The female EMT spoke into a walkie-talkie. I paid little attention until she said, "He's unresponsive. Weak pulse. I think we should airlift him to Stony Brook trauma …"

My heart dropped. I knew they only airlifted those in critical condition. Goosebumps grew on my shaky arms.

They hoisted the stretcher into the back of the ambulance.

"Daniel, stay strong. Stay strong, bro," I said, fighting off a second breakdown.

The back doors slammed shut and the ambulance tore across the field.

Dad rubbed his temples. He looked at me, then away.

"Do you want to ride there with us, sweetie?" Aunt Sue asked, her hand on my shoulder.

"I know the way," I said. "I'll meet you guys there."

CHAPTER 14

HEAVY RAIN ASSAULTED THE COROLLA'S WINDSHIELD. I switched the wiper blades to high. Rush-hour traffic on the Long Island Expressway sucked on normal days. Tonight it was torturous.

I merged into the right lane. I tried to clear my mind, to not think about what had happened. But how could I not? Daniel might have brain damage. He might be clinging to life. He might be dead.

The headlights carved a path on the Nichols Road exit ramp. I clamped my shaky hands onto the steering wheel. "God," I spoke aloud, "why are you doing this? What's wrong with you? Please let Daniel be okay. Please."

Rain lashed at the car's fogged-up windows. I struggled to decipher road signs. I knew this was the right road. We had passed that hospital on the way to an away game. But I didn't think the bus driver took us this far. Did I pass it? Shit!

I approached an exit for Route 27. Then I realized: Route 27 ran east and west along the southern part of Long Island.

"*Noooo!*" I screamed. "I'm headed south. Oh my god, I'm headed south! *Noooo!*"

I punched the dashboard, breaking the skin on my knuckles. I was supposed to be going north on Nichols!

I took the Route 27 West exit, intent on turning around as quickly as possible.

I drove the curvy exit ramp. Then I saw it.

Unmoving traffic.

A sea of taillights glowing red.

Emergency vehicle lights flashing in the distance.

How could there be an accident now? Oh no. Not now.

Stuck behind a pickup truck, I reached over to the passenger-side seat and frantically searched my bat bag for my cell phone. It didn't take me long to realize my phone wasn't in there. It was in my pants pocket. And my pants were in my locker.

My skin felt tingly, numb. Everybody was at the hospital. And I was stuck in this fucking car. "Help me. Help!"

Cranking the stereo, I shrieked. Nothing seemed real. I felt drugged, out of my mind.

A good forty-five minutes and a few nutty screams later, I drove past the accident. I took the first exit and made my way back to Nichols Road. North this time.

I cruised as fast as traffic would allow, puddles splashing the undercarriage of the car. I blew my horn and flashed the high beams at a hunk-of-junk green station wagon puttering along. The driver changed lanes. I pulled beside the old geezer, ready to uncork a verbal tirade, then realized how crazy I was being. His droopy eyes must have seen me a thousand times. Raising a wrinkly arm, he waved. I looked away and hit the gas. Cutting the wheel, I drifted across lanes then steered into the

Stony Brook Hospital entrance. I followed signs directing me to the emergency room parking.

The slanting rain drenched my baseball uniform when I dashed to the entrance. The automatic hospital doors parted. My wet sneakers squeaked on glossy flooring.

I hustled into the lobby, dripping water. "Andy!" Aunt Sue cried out, rushing over to me. "We were so worried about you. Are you okay?"

"Fine. How's Daniel?"

She hooked her arm around my waist. "We don't know yet, sweetie. Your dad's in there talking with a doctor now. We're waiting. Praying."

Lisa walked up to me, her pink mascara smudged on her cheeks. She hugged me. "How you holding up, Andy?"

"Okay," I lied. Pete and Coach both sat, rigid.

Hailey came over next, her face limp. She hugged me and wiped a tear sliding down her cheek.

Aunt Sue said all we could do was wait, but I couldn't stop pacing. My footfalls wore the waiting-room rug thin. I needed to know. As I strode purposely toward the registration desk, Dad pushed open an emergency room door.

"Dad," I said.

He looked like hell, eyes bloodshot and puffy. Holding the door open, he clutched his jittery left hand to waist of his pants.

A shiver shook me from head to toe. I knew my sucky life was about to change forever. For the worse.

He swallowed hard, motioned us in. "Family only."

I went in. Aunt Sue, Uncle John, Nathan and Craig followed.

Dad led us to an empty waiting room. He shut the door and brought a closed fist to his mouth. "The doctor said … they did everything … Danny's …" His mouth snarled up.

"What's going on?" I demanded. "What's wrong with Daniel?"

"He's dead," Dad snapped. "Danny's dead."

Ice filled my veins. My hands flew to my head. His words hit me like a Mack truck. "Don't lie, Dad. It's not funny. Where is he? I want to see my brother."

Dad crumpled onto a chair, his eyes squeezed shut.

Aunt Sue, sniffling, grabbed me by the shoulders. "I'm so sorry, Andy. I'm so sorry."

I shook her off. My tears broke loose. "No. It's not true. Where's my brother? They can save him. They need to try harder. Where is he?"

Nathan broke down, his palm muffling his hitching sobs.

I dropped to a knee, my hands splayed on the olive green-and-white flooring. "This isn't happening. It's not."

"I'm so sorry," Uncle John said.

I stood up, neck and shoulder muscles on fire with tension. I sat in the seat and gripped the back of my skull. We sat and nobody spoke. Nobody even moved.

I ripped off my cap, grabbed a fistful of my hair. "He's only sixteen. Sixteen!" I couldn't speak about him in the past tense.

Uncle John stood and scratched at his beard. "We're here for you. Whatever you guys need. I mean it. Anything."

Aunt Sue stood beside him. "Both of you are more than welcome to stay with us for as long as you need."

"I don't know what to do," Dad said.

I'd never heard Dad say that before. I looked up. He was staring at the floor.

"I can't believe this crap." I scraped my fingernails up and down my scalp. "I'm never going to see my brother alive again? He's going to be put in a box and stuck in the ground?"

"He's gone to a better place," Aunt Sue said.

Bullshit. What kind of God would let that happen? *Screw you, God. Screw you!*

Fighting a scream, I looked over at Craig, who leaned forward in his seat, his fingers steepled, eyes vacant. "It's crazy," he said. "Daniel was the nicest kid I've ever met. He'd do anything for anybody." He looked at me. "I'm sorry, man."

"It's my fault," I said, hand cupped to my forehead. "Daniel wanted to pitch a curveball. I changed his mind. That play would've never have happened if he threw a curveball. Never."

Dad closed his eyes, shook his head.

"No, Andy," Aunt Sue said, pointing at me. "It's nobody's fault. Not yours. Not the batter's. Nobody could have prevented what happened."

I rose to my feet. "I've gotta get out of here."

"I'll take you home, kid," Craig said.

"No," I snapped. "I need to be alone. Seriously. I just want to be alone right now."

Uncle John extended his hand. "Andy, maybe it's a good idea if—"

"Just leave me alone!" I yanked open the door and stormed out, strode down the hallway, opposite the direction I came in. I couldn't face Hailey and Lisa and Coach right now, or anybody.

For a second I thought about searching for Daniel in this godforsaken hospital. Finding his corpse. His shell. It would break me, though. Breathing fast and hard, I found a side exit and stepped into the fog and steady rain.

I drove my car without thinking, my mind a mess. Nerves wreaked havoc on my neck and shoulders. I prayed I was dreaming. That I'd wake up soon and everything would be back to normal.

I pulled into a Wal-Mart parking lot and parked near the back. If I thought I couldn't cry anymore, I was wrong. The tears wouldn't stop.

I pulled into our driveway a few minutes after midnight, the rain a drizzle now. I twisted the key out of the ignition and climbed out of the car, trudged up the steps and pushed open the front door.

Dad sat in his recliner, staring at a blank TV screen.

I kicked off my shoes.

He turned to me. "You okay?"

My gaze fell to the hardwood floor. "Yeah. You?"

"Yeah."

I removed my wet socks. "What are we going to do, Dad?"

He blew out a long breath. "I don't know, son. I don't know."

His empty eyes told the story. All that was good in his world was now gone. He was left with the dregs. We both were.

I headed to my bedroom and stopped in the doorway. I didn't want to go in. I didn't want to see Daniel's clothes. His books. His bed. But the other choice was to return to the living room.

Breathing irregularly, I stepped barefoot into the room and closed the door behind me.

I stripped out of my uniform, yanked down the blinds, and killed the light. I slugged my body underneath the covers.

There would be no peaceful sleep, but I didn't feel much like moving. My mind raced at warp speed. Tomorrow, everything would return to normal. Daniel would be there slopping gel on his hair, talking to me about Hailey. About baseball.

This all had to be a nightmare. It had to be.

At some point during the night, my mind surrendered and I dozed off. Whatever sleep I managed didn't last long. I dreamed of Daniel trapped in his coffin, panicked, calling for me to help him out. Men in black suits slid a closed casket into a furnace of flames.

I woke up in a cold sweat, hands clutching my blanket. I looked over at Daniel's bed, still neatly made.

My insides clenched. Raw pain. I coiled into the fetal position and rocked my head. I didn't want to be there. I wasn't so sure I wanted to be alive.

I looked at my alarm clock: 4:07 a.m. My skin prickled. I scratched at my legs and arms like a madman.

I swung my feet off the bed, heart pounding. I choked down air. Not a panic attack. Not now.

I put on some sweats, stuffed my feet into sneakers, and walked out the front door.

It was no longer raining. A slight haze rose from the wet road. A street lamp hummed.

I walked down the block. I didn't know where I was going. I didn't care.

My shoes slapped the wet pavement and I picked up the pace. Soon I was jogging. Then running. Then sprinting. Breath clouded in front of my face. My legs throbbed. But I kept going until my body couldn't push on anymore.

I stopped and sat on a curb, sucking wind, thinking about Daniel. About better times. About the hell my life was queued up to become.

CHAPTER 15

DAD PULLED INTO AN OPEN SPOT IN THE PARKING LOT and silenced the Malibu. I snapped off my seatbelt. "This is really happening, isn't it?"

His face tightened. He nodded.

Through the foggy car window, the sign read: Maloney Funeral Home. I'd have preferred to stay in the car. To not go in there and see Daniel's body. To not have reality kick me in the head.

Dad straightened his necktie. "Got a call from a scout looking to speak to Daniel this morning. Guess the moron doesn't read the papers."

"I'm sorry," I muttered. The major newspapers covered Daniel's death. I couldn't bring myself to read any of them.

Dad blew out a breath. "Let's go."

I climbed out of the car, my back, neck and shoulders aching from the unrelenting weight of anxiety. My tired eyes burned. My empty stomach grumbled.

A golden morning sun crowned the sprawling funeral home. I buttoned up the front of my black suit jacket while Dad led the way up the brick walkway. He held open a large white door. I entered, forcing myself to be strong.

A well-dressed man with a gray handlebar mustache gave us a warm smile. I stuffed my shaky hands into my pockets.

"Up this way," Dad said softly.

Walking stiffly, I gazed at the nameplate above an open double doorway. "Daniel Lembo." My heart ripped.

Dad entered, his head tipped forward.

I followed, and when we were almost to the white coffin, something gargled in my chest. I swiveled my eyes to Daniel. His hands folded over his chest. *I can't be looking at my dead brother. I can't.*

"You coming up?" Dad asked.

"I'm good back here for now." I stepped behind neat rows of unfilled brown chairs.

Dad approached the casket and knelt on the pew. He touched Daniel's hand and sniffled. Then he wept. The first time I'd ever seen him cry.

I thought I knew pain before. I knew nothing.

In the downstairs bathroom of the funeral home, I splashed cold water on my face. Upstairs was packed. A lot more people than the afternoon session. Family. Friends. Teachers. Students. The entire baseball team. People I sort of knew. People I didn't know at all.

I shut off the faucet and regarded myself in the mirror. No amount of cleaning could scrub away the guilt. If I'd just listened to Daniel and let him throw his damn curveball, none of this would be happening.

I finished up in the bathroom and entered the downstairs lounge.

Coach lumbered over to me, dropped his bear claw on my shoulder. "I'm sorry for your loss, Andy."

"Thanks, Coach. That means a lot."

"Your brother was a great baseball player. An even better person."

"I know it."

"I'm sure you'll be taking some time off. But if you decide to come back on the team, your starting position will be waiting for you."

I looked at the floor. "Thanks, Coach. But baseball? Those days are over."

"I understand. We'll miss you. My door's always open if you want to talk."

"Thanks."

I went upstairs and looked into the room where Daniel lay.

A woman, thirtyish, approached me, her black satin dress hugging her wide hips. "I'm very sorry."

I nodded, unable to place her. "Thanks."

"I'm Pam Hanes. I believe you and your brother saved my son's life. Pulled little Johnny up from the tracks?"

I half-smiled, recalling Daniel's leap and rescue. Super-Dan.

Pam bridged her fingers. "My mother isn't one to exaggerate. I know what you guys did was truly heroic. Thank you."

I scratched my forehead. "No problem. Daniel was the real hero. I'm just glad your son is okay."

Water glazed her eyes. "You'll never know how grateful I am. I don't know what I would have … Johnny's my world. Not many would've done what you guys did. May your brother rest in peace. May God bless you both."

I nodded. "I appreciate it."

I walked over to Aunt Sue. She rubbed my back with one hand, pointed to a photo displayed on a table with her other. "Look at the two of you here."

Daniel and me down on a knee, matching Little League uniforms. A gapped-tooth smile on Daniel's face, his Rawlings baseball glove cupped to his knee. Me with a serious, closed-mouth look. Typical.

I swallowed over a lump in my throat. Even then, as a third grader, Daniel was better than most kids playing on the middle school team.

"He was something special," Aunt Sue said.

I saw a photo of me, lying on top of Daniel, the two of us sledding down a hill. I drew in a breath and looked away.

"Why don't you come up with me?" she said, motioning toward the casket. "Say goodbye."

I sighed, let my shoulders slump. "I'll do it by myself. Just got to screw up the courage."

I circled around to Daniel's casket, my hands nervously bouncing on my thighs. Pressure built behind my eyes.

I knelt in front of the casket. "Nothing's gonna be the same without you, bro," I whispered, a tear running down the scarred side of my face. "Nothing."

I took his batting glove out of my back pocket. The one Grandpa Bill gave him. The magic glove. I tucked it into the casket. "I'm gonna miss you so much. So damn much."

I dried my tears with my sleeve then stood and walked away, not able to bear the pain of being there any longer. I walked outside the funeral home, desperate for fresh air. I found a bench on the front lawn and prayed for Daniel. Prayed to a God I didn't fully believe in. Prayed for some kind of mercy.

I leaned forward, my elbows on my knees. A petite, middle-age woman puffed on a cigarette over by the funeral home porch. She was looking directly at me, smoke leaking from her pursed lips. I couldn't see her clearly; she stood just out of the light. I looked away, then back at her. Her sunken eyes were still on me.

Something about the way she stood looked familiar. Crazy, but her stance was something like the picture Dad still had of The Bitch.

She squashed her cigarette with her black shoe then walked down the brick path toward me. She entered the glow from a lamppost and I got a clear view. A mole below her chin. Skin, pale as porcelain, pulled tight across high cheekbones. Freckles splattered across the bridge of her nose.

I didn't remember much about my mother. But I recalled the mole. And I'd browsed enough photo albums to know.

Her high heels clicked against the brick walkway.

My heart twisted, forming a chunk of lead in my throat.

"Andy?"

She stood before me, her eyes laced with guilt. She knew the answer. Not many people had a scar across half of their face.

I found my footing. "That's me." Anger, rich and hot, choked me, kept me from saying more.

"My, how you've grown," she said. Her eyes were adrift, her head shaking. "I couldn't believe when I heard. I'm sorry."

"You should be. Daniel was a great kid. You missed out."

She shook her head some more. "I know I've made mistakes. I know."

"Didn't you get Daniel's letters?"

"I did."

I scoffed. "The kid always remembered to send you a birthday card. He just wanted to hear from you. Why didn't you write back?"

"I don't know. I was in a dark place. I was really messed up for a long time."

"Why are you here now?"

"Daniel's my son. Regardless of what you might think, you two were always on my mind."

I folded my arms. "On your mind? We haven't heard from you in a decade."

"I can't change the past."

I pulled my blazer closed. Something in my stomach twisted. "You gave up on us. You've got some nerve showing up here now."

"I don't blame you for being angry at me."

"Listen, I have way too much going on now to deal with … I need some time alone. The priest will be saying prayers soon. Everybody's inside."

Her features pulled downward. "Okay. Maybe things can be different between us."

I looked away and rubbed my forehead.

She walked off.

I lowered myself to the bench, my body ready to combust with bottled emotions.

Daniel's tombstone cast a shadow that reached the tips of my sneakers. I knelt and placed a David Wright baseball card beside a bouquet of yellow and white flowers that Aunt Sue had brought the day before.

They stuck Daniel in the ground on a Friday. I was able to keep my composure for most of that horrific day. Not when I went to put a red rose on his closed casket, though. I just couldn't release the stem. My brave facade crumbled. I broke down.

Mom didn't show up at the church or at the burial. She said she was going to come. There wouldn't be a new beginning between us. I said a final goodbye to two people that day.

I stood up and looked across the overcast sky, the endless rows of headstones. My insides felt ripped. "I'm so sorry, bro. I should've listened to you. It was my fault. Mine. This isn't the way things were supposed to play out. You were supposed to be famous. Go pro. You were supposed to break pitching records ... I don't know how I'm going to carry on without you."

I wiped snot from under my nose. "Why did this happen? Why?"

CHAPTER 16

THE CABLE BOX FLASHED 1:34 A.M. I TOSSED AND TURNED on the plastic-covered couch, my legs twined in a sheet. My anxiety was off the charts, hive breakouts and all. Whatever little sleep I managed to catch occurred right there on the couch. I couldn't sleep in my room. Dad said he'd take care of getting rid of Daniel's stuff. That was two weeks ago. Yet Daniel's stuff remained. Honestly, my room gave me the heebie-jeebies.

The front door swung open, and my heart skipped a beat.

Dad stumbled inside the house, his eyes red-rimmed. Dad was not a drinker. But Jack Daniel's must have introduced himself tonight.

I swung my socked feet to the floor. "Hey," I said. "No work tonight?"

Dad ran his fingers through his disheveled hair. "Didn't I tell you not to sleep out here?"

"No. When'd you tell me that?"

He kicked off his sneakers and untucked his T-shirt. "I wanna watch the game. Go sleep in your room."

"What game? Are you drunk?"

He pointed his shaky finger at me. "You keep your mouth shut. Hear me?"

Every muscle in my body pulled tight. "Yeah. I see where this conversation is headed."

He took a few wobbly steps. "Place is a freakin' mess. Ever heard of a broom? You're a goddamn slob."

"Nice." I said, anger swelling in my chest.

"When you gettin' your lazy ass back to school?"

"Not this year," I snapped.

"Find yourself a job then. Or 'nother place to live."

"Screw off."

Dad turned toward me, his eyes narrowed to slits. "Know what? Daniel was a winner at everything. You? Nothing but a *loser*."

"Good. Like father like son."

He staggered into the kitchen. I marched in after him.

Dad threw a chair to the floor. "Can't put a fucking dish away? You stupid or something?"

"What's your problem? Mom left you. Daniel's dead. You want me out of your life, too? You got it."

"Good. Go. Who needs you?"

I stormed into my room, snarled, and screamed the pain out. I flipped Daniel's bed over. My muscles straining, I slid his twin mattress out of my room. "This is going in your room. You sleep with your dead son's mattress."

"Don't you dare!"

Adrenaline surging through my veins, I put my shoulder to a side of the mattress and drove hard with my legs. I bent the mattress through the doorway to Dad's bedroom. Forced it in.

Then I rammed it into one of his walls. The vibrations knocked The Bat and its pedestal off a shelf.

"You ugly son of a bitch," Dad said, entering the room. "Get ta fuck outta my room!"

I held back tears. "I hate you."

"I hate *you*!" He picked the bat up off the floor, a large muscle flexing in his neck. He sledgehammered the bat on the edge of a solid oak desk. One hit. Two hits. The third hit cracked the barrel of the bat. He dropped to his knees, his hands clenching the bat's handle.

I ran into my room and rifle-shot items into a suitcase. Luggage in tow, I fled through the front door.

What the hell was going on? This wasn't happening, was it?

My head throbbing, I hurled the suitcase into the backseat of my car and slammed the door. I got in and fired up the engine.

I sped out down my block and out to the Long Island Expressway, where I tried to push the pedal through the floor. Nobody would care if I were dead.

I screamed until my lungs ached, "Why? Why is this happening to me? What did I do to deserve this? What?"

Something stabbed at my ribcage. *I'm having a heart attack. My God.*

I swallowed hard. "I can't breathe. Oh, no. Don't. No panic attack."

I slowed, merged into the right lane, exited. At the first intersection, I swung into a Best Western.

I parked in the back, away from the other cars, slid my hand underneath my shirt and placed it over my heart. *I need to go the emergency room. Something's not right. Nothing's right.*

My right shoulder twitched involuntarily. My feet felt numb. Tingly sensations ran down my arms.

Stop it. Nothing is wrong. It's anxiety. Just my goddamn anxiety.

I closed my eyes and tucked my head between my knees, my head pressed to the steering wheel. Images of Daniel's last pitch replayed in my mind. The ball coming out of his hands. The ball coming off the bat. The way he staggered and crumpled.

After several minutes of breathing into my leg, I felt more in control. I lifted my head and coughed out a breath.

I took out my cell phone and dialed Nathan. He didn't answer. I tried again.

"Hull-lo." Nathan sounded half-asleep.

"Nathan." My hand shook as I held the phone up to my ear.

"Andy? You okay?"

"No. I'm not. I'm buggin'."

"What's going on? Where are you?"

"In my car. Smithtown, I think."

"Are you all right?"

"My dad's drunk. We just got into a huge fight. I can't go back there. You think I can come over and stay the night? Maybe longer."

"Sure. You know my mom's been asking you."

"I just don't want to be a bother."

"Dude, you're family. You need us to come get you?"

"No, I'm fine. I'll be there in a few."

"Okay. You sure you're okay to drive?"

"I'm good. Thanks, man."

"Be careful. See you in a bit."

I closed my phone and shut my eyes. I prayed for the pain to go away. I prayed for this nightmare to be over. I didn't know how much more of this I could take.

A little after 3 a.m., I parked behind Craig's car and climbed out. Struggling to keep my eyelids open, I carried my suitcase up the paved walkway. A porch light clicked on.

I knocked on the front door, two taps with my middle knuckle. Buster barked.

Aunt Sue, in a robe and slippers, pulled open the door. "Hi, Andy."

"Hi," I said, entering the house. I put my suitcase down on the glossy hardwood floor.

Nathan stood in the foyer, his arms crossed. "You look tired, man."

I petted Buster, a brown and white spaniel. He was jumping up on me. "Haven't been able to sleep much. Sorry to wake you guys."

"It's okay, sweetie," Aunt Sue said, pulling the silk belt at her waist. "I have everything set up for you in the guest room."

"Thanks. I appreciate it."

"Nathan tells me your dad's been drinking tonight. Is that right?"

"Yeah, he came staggering in after midnight. Then he went off on me. Said some mean stuff. Then he really lost it. He broke the signed bat."

"Your grandfather was a nasty drunk. Your father gets it from him."

I looked at her in disbelief. "Grandpa B? The Big B drank?"

"Not in his later years. As kids, though, your dad and I used to ... it wasn't pretty."

I massaged my forehead. "I can't believe all this is happening. Dad really pissed me off tonight."

"Drinking changes people. Is tonight the first night he's come home drunk?"

"Far as I know."

"I'm sorry, Andy. I'm sure the booze was responsible for whatever he did or said."

"I don't know. I heard somewhere ... sometimes the truth

comes out when you're smashed. I feel like he blames me for Daniel's death."

"He said that?"

"No. I just know. He hates me."

"Your father can be a tough person to live with. I should know. But he loves you very much. Don't ever think he doesn't."

"He's never told me he loves me. Not once."

"Andy—"

"I think I'll just crash now if that's okay. I'm done for tonight."

"Sure, honey. Follow me."

"I'm heading up," Nathan said around a yawn. "G'night, Andy."

"Night, pal. Sorry for waking you."

Aunt Sue flicked on the light in the guest bedroom. "Not a Marriott. But I hope this will do."

"It's great," I said. And it was. A made-up twin bed. Plush carpet. A matching wooden nightstand and dresser. Some closet space. Clean.

"Give me a holler if you need anything."

"Thanks." I set my suitcase down by the closet. "Is it okay if this turns into an extended stay?"

"Stay as long as you'd like."

"Cool."

She tugged the hem of her robe so it covered her knees. "Try and get some rest, Andy. Your body needs to recharge."

"I'll try."

"Sweet dreams. See you in morning."

"'Kay. Goodnight."

She pulled the door closed behind her. I sat on the edge of the twin bed, rubbing my forehead.

After a while, I stepped out of my sneakers. I unzipped my suitcase, and located the bottle of Benadryl. I'd been taking a few capsules each night to help me get some shuteye. Tonight needed a third dose.

I pressed my palm down on the cap and spun the top open. I stared into the pill bottle. *I can end it now. The pain. The awful thoughts. Everything.*

I tapped out two pills. Then tipped the bottle more, the pills piling into my cupped hand. I fantasized about going for it. About relief.

Yeah right. Won't happen. Once a pussy, always a pussy. Probably screw it up anyway. End up a damn vegetable or something.

I looked at the door. Part of me feared somebody walking in and finding me with the pills. Part of me wanted the door to open.

I let all but two of the pills slide out of my hand and back into the bottle. I popped the two pills in my mouth and chased it with Gatorade, killed the light, and slid into bed.

The negative thoughts hounded me as I rocked under my covers.

There's no denying it anymore. I need help. The sooner the better.

CHAPTER 17

I PERCHED ON DR. STEWARD'S BROWN LEATHER COUCH. SHORT, labored breaths stabbed at my windpipe.

She closed the blinds.

"Thanks for seeing me, short notice and all," I said.

"You're welcome, dear." She walked toward me, the heels of her black shoes padding softly against the brown carpet.

She had paid her respects at Daniel's wake. Last Monday, we had our first session since Daniel's death. This morning, I called her and clued her in to the fireworks hours earlier with Dad. She insisted I come in and talk it over. No charge.

My hands bounced on my thighs while she sat in a black swivel chair, crossed her left leg over her right. "How are you, Andy?"

"I've seen better days." I told her about all that had happened. She listened intently. Asked questions. Jotted notes.

"I'm sorry you're going through all this," she said, sounding like she meant it. "Are you getting much sleep at night?"

"Sleep? What's that?"

She tucked gray locks of hair behind her ear. "How's your anxiety?"

I shook my head. "Pretty bad. My mind doesn't stop. I can't relax. I can't just think about nothing."

"You're grieving, Andy. People feel grief in many ways. They handle it differently, too."

"Sometimes I feel somewhat back to my old self. But mostly I feel sad and like crap. Maybe I need to start taking meds or something."

"Meds are always an option. But maybe we can increase our therapy sessions first, and explore the medication options down the road."

I nodded.

"You have fight. You're going to be just fine."

My lips pressed together, I gulped.

She peered over her narrow glasses. "I'd like to talk to you about school. Is that okay?"

"What's to talk about? I'm not going back."

"Ever?"

"I don't know. For what?"

"Andy, you're a few weeks away from graduating high school. It would be a real shame for you to quit now."

"What's a high school degree gonna get me? I'm not going to college. I'm destined to work at some dead-end job. I'm going to end up just like my dad."

"Your life isn't predetermined. You make your life what it is. When you were a kid, what was your big dream?"

I scratched the back of my head. "I wanted to announce baseball games. Silly, right? Daniel and I used to mute the sound on the Mets games and call it ourselves. It was a hoot."

"I'm sure it was. Do you think Daniel would want you to graduate high school and make the most of your life?"

I closed my wet eyes and imagined Daniel in his baseball uniform, cheering me on. "Yeah. Absolutely. He'd tell me to get my butt back on the baseball team, too."

"Know what I believe? I believe you can get that diploma. I believe you can do anything you put your heart to."

Daniel always said stuff like that to me. Said I could do anything I wanted with my life. Said he could, too. But he was wrong, wasn't he? And with Daniel gone, there was no family to even say those words to me anymore.

Dad's car wasn't parked in our driveway when I was on my way back to Nathan's from Dr. Steward's office. So I stopped in and packed a big suitcase with other stuff I'd failed to pack when I bolted earlier.

I got back to my car in a hurry, drove the rest of the block but parked by the curb. I wanted Dad to see my car at Aunt Sue's house. I wanted him to know his days of treating me like a piece of shit were over.

My suitcase thumping against my leg, I walked past Aunt Sue's new Jeep Cherokee, the lone car parked in the long driveway.

I climbed the porch steps. *Do I knock? Just go in?*

Through a windowpane on one side of the front door, I watched Aunt Sue winding up a vacuum cord. I rang the doorbell.

Buster yapped. Aunt Sue opened the door. "Andy, there's no need to knock."

I stepped inside, the aroma of home cooking flooding my senses. "Yeah, I wasn't sure. This is all a little weird."

"Please, feel at home."

I petted Buster. "Something smells good."

"Pork chops. You like those, right?"

"Yep."

"Good. I talked to your dad. He knows you're going to stay here a while. He said to tell you he was sorry."

Bullshit. Dad doesn't apologize. "He should be sorry. Did he explain why he wigged out and destroyed The Bat?"

"He didn't. I didn't press him."

I huffed. "Do Craig and Nathan have a game tonight?"

"No, just practice. They should be home, sixish."

I hoisted my suitcase. "Cool. I'm going to get things set up in the room."

"Okay, sweetie. Let me know if you need anything."

After dragging my suitcase next to my other one, I sat on the side of the bed. I kicked off my shoes and stared blankly at my fingers, trying to clear my thoughts, but my mind kept replaying twisted images of the funeral.

My body felt hollow as I laid down and pulled a blanket over my head. I closed my burning eyes and thought of better days. Days when Daniel and I had a blast doing stupid shit, like building forts in our backyard, playing video games until the wee hours, and having Super Soaker wars. I missed our stupid conversations. His stupid laugh. His subtle arrogance.

A knock at the door snapped me out of a deep sleep.

"Andy," Nathan said. "Dinnertime."

"'Kay." I pressed my blanket to my chest. "Be right there."

I looked at my alarm clock: 6:54 P.M.

My stomach grumbling, I forced myself out of bed and walked lifelessly to the dining room. Aunt Sue had set a glass pan filled with bubbling glazed pork chops in the center of the table. Steam rose from broccoli, corn, and mashed potatoes already dished onto plates.

Uncle John, Craig, and Nathan, seated at the table, turned toward me.

"Hey," I said.

"Hey, what's up, kid?" Craig asked.

"Not too much."

Uncle John poured himself a glass of lemonade. "We're glad you'll be spending some time with us."

"Thanks for having me." I sat in a wooden chair and pulled up to the table.

Aunt Sue stabbed a pork chop and placed it on my plate. "One or two?"

"One's good, for now."

I wasn't used to being served. I wasn't used to any of this. Caring parents. A home-cooked meal. A clean, spacious house.

"Pass the applesauce," Nathan asked.

Uncle John slid the jar down to Nathan.

I worked a knife through my pork chop. This was their family time. What the hell was I doing here?

"Hey, Mom, you wash my uniform?" Craig asked.

"Don't I always?"

Craig smirked.

"How's the team doing?" I asked.

"Good. We're 18 and 4. Still in first." He wiped a corner of his mouth with a napkin.

"Playoffs start next week," Nathan said.

"Good luck. How's Joey been catching?"

"He hasn't," Nathan said. "Coach benched him. Brought Matt Turrow up from JV. He's a good catcher. Has a good arm."

"Not as good as you," Craig added, pointing his fork at me.

I flashed a smile. Craig had been different toward me since Daniel died. Nicer. But it felt forced, unnatural. Like he was scared to push me over the edge or something.

I looked down at my plate. "I've been thinking about finishing school this year. Redoing senior year next year isn't going to work for me."

Aunt Sue smiled. "Good for you, Andy."

"Maybe as early as next week. I don't know. Finals are coming up. I'm not doing anyone any good staring at four walls all day."

Still chewing a bit, Nathan said, "Lisa's been asking about you."

I held my eyes closed for a second. "Yeah. I've been bad about returning her calls. Been a hermit to the world."

"It's understandable," Aunt Sue said. "But life does go on. Daniel would want you to move on."

"I know he would."

After dinner, Nathan asked me to watch the Mets game with him in the living room. I just wanted to go back to sleep. But I didn't want to seem like a difficult houseguest either, so I said yes.

I sat at the short end of their L-shaped couch and gazed at the flat-screen TV. "Who they playing?"

"St. Louis," Nathan said.

Uncle John joined us. He sat in a recliner and cracked open a beer. "Mets are hot right now."

News to me. I hadn't been following them. I hadn't been keeping up with much of anything.

The Mets were down 1–0 a half-inning in.

As the leadoff batter waved his bat, my mind looped thoughts of a comebacker. The pitcher bloodied, dropping to his knees on the mound.

In the bottom half of the third inning, I decided to call it quits on watching the game. My neck was tense as hell. I couldn't think clearly. I wasn't enjoying the game at all. So I told the guys I was tired and retreated to the guestroom.

Lying on my bed in the dark, I could still hear the TV. The game I once loved. The game I couldn't bear to watch anymore.

If I couldn't handle a simple baseball game on television, how was I going to manage school?

CHAPTER 18

I CRANKED OUT PUSHUPS, ONE AFTER THE OTHER, MOUTH snarled, teeth grinding. After a long grunt, my wobbly arms gave way and my chest thumped onto the carpeted floor in the guestroom. Forty.

In the five days after I moved in with my aunt and uncle, I'd spent most of my time alone in this room behind a closed door. A lot of thinking. Missing Daniel. A lot. I even missed Dad some. Dad and I hadn't spoken since our meltdown. Aunt Sue was bent on me calling him. No thanks. He was the one who acted like a dick. He was the one who should apologize. If there was anyone who could save our damaged relationship, it was him. If he even wanted to.

I hopped to my feet and donned a blue Polo shirt.

Today's the day, I thought. *School or bust.* It was time to make something of my haphazard life. If for no other reason than to spite Dad.

I stepped into my sneakers, grabbed my backpack and exited the guestroom.

Craig, seated at the kitchen table, shoveled Fruit Loops into his mouth.

"Morning," I said, tucking the shirt into jeans.

"Hey," he said.

My stomach did that flipping thing. "I *so* could just crawl back in bed right now."

He lifted the bowl to his mouth and downed the milk. "Only a few weeks to go, champ. Then it's goodbye, high school."

"Yeah, I guess."

"Hungry?"

"I'm good." I'd eaten and showered earlier, before anyone was up. Making myself at home here was still a work-in-progress.

I sat down and pressed my sweaty palms on the table. "I hope I'm ready to go back."

"You got it," he said. "Wanna ride with Nathan and me?"

"Nah. You guys got practice tonight. Taking the bus home is the last thing I need to do to myself."

He narrowed his eyes. "You should come down to practice. Play with us again."

"You're kidding, right?"

"No. Not at all. I'd much rather pitch to you than Turrow. We could use you for the playoffs."

I huffed. "I'm not wired anything like that. I'd probably have some kind of nervous breakdown on the field."

He pushed his bowl aside. "You and Daniel always dreamed of winning a championship, no?"

"Yeah," I said, sharper than I intended. "Together."

His forehead wrinkled. "Daniel's not coming back, Andy."

"No shit."

He looked away, then back at me. "Daniel wouldn't want

you to hang up your cleats. That's all I'm saying. He wouldn't want you to give up on your dream. On his dream."

"It's not going to happen. Sorry. I just can't."

"The kid loved baseball. You love baseball."

I released a deep, tremulous breath. "Baseball took my brother's life. What's to love?"

"What about Dale Earnhardt? He died racing a car. A race his son was in. That didn't stop his son from continuing to race cars."

"That's different."

"How?"

My blood boiled. "It just is. So stop."

Nathan walked into the kitchen, mussing with collar on his shirt. "Stop what?"

"Nothing." I checked the time on my cell phone. "I'm gonna head out. I'll see you guys at school."

"'Kay," Nathan said.

Craig gave me a soldier salute. "Later," he said.

I went outside, the low sun shining in my eyes like a flashlight. The hot, humid, late-May air slammed my face. I walked out to the street and climbed in the Corolla. Turned the key in the ignition. A click. A sputter. Then nothing.

Not now. C'mon.

I turned the key again. The engine turned over.

I cruised down side roads, steering with two hands.

Stopped at a red light, I looked over at the high school. The baseball fields. A bubble of panic burst in my chest, rippled through my insides.

The light turned green. My foot tingling, I pressed down on the pedal.

My mind went blank as I reached the entrance gates to the school, and I kept driving. *Shit. Why didn't I turn in?*

I squeezed the steering wheel, my knuckles going white. *Dad's right. I don't have it in me. I'm a loser. Always will be.*

I kept driving, not knowing where the heck I was headed. I ended up parked at the Smith Haven Mall, about a half hour from the school.

I killed the engine and tilted the rearview mirror down. Not a pretty sight. Dark circles stamped my droopy eyes. Overgrown bangs. A big zit on my chin that I hadn't noticed before.

I looked over at the empty passenger seat. "What's wrong with me, bro? Why can't I be brave like you? Super-Dan."

Water glazed my eyes. "I miss you, man. I don't wanna put on a happy face and pretend everything's okay. 'Cause it's not. Everything sucks."

I reclined my seat and closed my eyes. I thought of the night Daniel and I went to a Minor League Redwings game in Rochester. It was about six months before we moved downstate. At the stadium, they had a spot over by the food vendors where fans could pitch a baseball into a rubber mat that resembled a catcher. A staff member clocked the pitcher's speed with a radar gun. They kept track of speeds by age category.

Daniel waited in line and paid his dollar. A worker, fortyish with slicked-back hair, handed him a baseball. "Age?"

"Fifteen."

The worker pointed his radar gun at the mat. "How fast you think you can throw?"

"Eighty-five."

The man chuckled, his round belly bouncing. "No, really."

Daniel massaged the baseball. "Eighty-five."

"Hey, Rodney," the worker said. "Get a load of this kid. He's fifteen and says he's going to eighty-five miles per hour. Did you know we had Roger Clemens' son in attendance?"

Rodney laughed. So did others standing on line.

Daniel wound up, snarled, and fired the ball. The laughing stopped. Jaws hung loose.

I was sure his speed was still the high-water mark.

I leaned forward and powered on the radio. I eased back, Eric Clapton soothing me.

With eyes closed, I dredged up another memory. This one from when I graduated middle school. I was nervous as hell, waiting to go up on the stage and get my diploma and shake hands with Principal Richards. All those eyes on me. Principal Richards read the names alphabetically. A lot of the kids got big roars from the crowd when it was their turn. I expected my name to yield a sea of silence. But when Principal Richards called out Andy Lembo, there was one voice that boomed.

"Yeah, you go, Andy! *Woot! Woot!*" Daniel screamed, his fist pumping.

That was Daniel. Always there for me. Always cheering me on. No matter how much of a screw-up I was.

I sat up and twisted the key in the ignition. Giving up was not an option. Not today. Steering with my left hand, I checked the time on my cell phone. I'd never make first period. No need to rush.

I found a spot in the school parking lot and got out of the car before I could convince myself otherwise. Sweat beaded on my forehead. My heart raced.

I looped my thumb in front of my pocket while I strolled past the parked buses. Holding my book bag at my side, I marched up the concrete steps and through the main entrance.

The gleaming hallway reeked of Clorox. I could have barfed right then. No need to even gag myself.

The bell rang. Students filled the hallway. Stares came from all directions. Some subtle. Some obvious. For sure, everyone had heard about what happened to Daniel. How could they not? It was all over the news, even the national news.

I thought about taking the long way to my locker to avoid passing Daniel's. Instead, I rounded the bend in the hallway. My eyes snapped to it. I pictured him leaning back, a goofy smile on his face. I lowered my gaze to my sneakers.

I stopped at my locker, spun the dial to 23. Shit. *What the hell's my combo?*

"Hey, Andy." A hand clapped my shoulder.

"Pete."

"Glad to see you back."

My lips flirted with a smile. "Wish I was glad to be back."

Daniel's death seemed to hit Pete hard. He was a mess at the funeral.

"How've you been holding up?" Pete asked.

"Doing okay. You?"

"Good."

I cleared my throat. "It's cool the team has top seed in the playoffs."

"Yeah, that's always a plus."

He scratched under his ear. "You coming back to play for us?"

"Nah. I'm done."

"Yeah. I understand."

"Heard Turrow's doing a good job behind the plate."

"He's all right."

I set my book bag on the floor and folded my arms. "Do me a favor. Take the championship. Win it for Daniel."

His lips twisted upward. "We'll try, bud. I'll catch up with you later. Take care of yourself."

"Will do. Later."

Pete walked off. I turned and spun the dial, this time remembering the combo.

After gathering my stuff, I headed to second period. Biology.

"Hi, Andy," Mr. Rice said from behind at his desk, gazing at me through bottle-thick glasses. "Welcome back."

"Thanks." I took a seat in the third row of the empty classroom. I opened my five-subject notebook and feigned interest in month-old notes.

He walked over to me. "I'm sorry for your loss."

"Thanks."

"I'm available for extra help after school if you'd like. Finals are coming."

I chewed on my lower lip. "Might just take you up on that."

Mr. Rice was my History teacher, too. I was barely passing both classes. If I wanted to graduate, I couldn't afford to bomb finals.

Students filed in and settled into seats.

Mr. Rice rolled up the cuffs on his shirt, revealing gray-haired forearms. He straightened a stack of papers on his desk. "Good morning, class. Some of you will be glad to know your tests are graded. Some, not so much. Overall, the scores averaged higher than the previous one. So the curve won't be as steep. Twelve points will be added on this time."

After he handed out the marked tests, he walked over to the Smart Board and started the lesson.

Through the first half of class, I stayed focused and took meticulous notes. Until the unwanted thoughts swept through my mind. Thoughts of me passing out. Thoughts of my heart giving out on me. Thoughts of Mattelson hitting that comebacker. I wrote faster, concentrating on the words Mr. Rice spewed. So much so, my temples pulsated.

With about ten minutes remaining in the class, there came a loud dinging sound. The fire alarm. "Let's go, everyone," Mr. Rice said. "Exit down the hallway to your right."

Tucking my notebook under my arm, I joined the flow of students in the hallway. Strobe lights flashed. The alarm blared.

Outside, my ears continued to ring. I scanned the landscape stretching back to the road and found a spot to stand over by a guardrail in the parking lot. I could almost feel the eyes on me. Holing up in the guestroom seemed like a nice option.

Everyone seemed to enjoy the unexpected recess. I just wanted to go back to class and do my time.

"Andy." Lisa appeared from out of the crowd, her eyes large and round. "You're back."

I bit down on my lip. "Hey, Lisa."

She took decisive strides and stopped in front of me. "How are you doing? Everyone's been so worried about you."

I felt my cheeks flush. "I'm okay. How 'bout yourself?"

Glitter sparkled on her eyelids. "Holding up. Your brother would be so proud of you. Coming back and graduating. *I'm* proud of you."

My tight face felt like it was cracking, but I managed a smile. "Thanks. I have to get my grades up or I won't be graduating."

"I can help you study if you want."

"You'll be sorry you agreed to this. I'm pretty dumb."

"No. You're not. You're going to do great."

I blew out a breath. "How's Hailey been handling everything?"

"It's been rough on her. She's out sick today. Actually, she's been out sick a lot lately."

"Daniel really loved her. I know they only went out a couple weeks. And he wasn't one to say so. But I could tell."

"She loved him, too. Still does. The whole thing's just so sad."

I looked down, scraped my sneaker over the sandy pavement. "Life can be a real bitch sometimes."

"It sure can."

Fire engines roared into the parking lot. My mind looped thoughts of the ambulance and police SUV racing down to the field.

"You think it's a real fire?" I asked.

"Nah. Seniors have been pulling a lot of stupid pranks lately. Either that or it's a scheduled fire drill."

I continued to shoot the breeze with Lisa. About a half hour later, a teacher with a frizzy black shawl told us it was safe to go back inside.

"Any time you want to talk, Andy. I mean it. Any time. Just give me a call. We're all going to get through this. Together."

Striding toward the school, alongside Lisa, I said, "One day at a time … one day at a time."

CHAPTER 19

M R. RICE STUFFED A *WALL STREET JOURNAL* INTO HIS briefcase then walked over to me, his back slightly hunched, his bushy eyebrows arched. "It's been a pleasure, Andy. You worked hard and caught up quickly. You're going do just fine on Regents next week."

I stood up from my desk and shook his hand. "I hope you're right. I appreciate all the extra time you put in helping me out."

He nudged his glasses up on his nose. "You're welcome. Good luck."

I hoisted my book bag. "Thanks. Have a nice weekend, sir."

"You too, Andy."

My chin high, I strode down the vacant school hallway, past Daniel's locker. *I gave it my all, bro. For you.* I certainly didn't put in the extra effort to please Dad. He wouldn't care.

Not that I've talked to him. Three weeks and counting. No phone call. Nothing. Yeah, he gets updates from Aunt Sue on how I'm doing. But that's not a conversation.

I zipped through my locker combination and went through the ritual of putting in what I didn't need to take home, and pulling out what I did need. Schoolwork had been my outlet, an escape from thoughts I'd rather not have rattling around in my brain.

I pulled out my Biology workbook and stuffed it into my book bag, slammed my locker and gave the lock a spin, then headed out a side door. My lungs drew in the thick, sticky June air. A gold sun peeked over the horizon.

Heading to my car, I made a huge mistake: I glanced down the hill. At the baseball field, where my former teammates were practicing.

They won Leagues on Wednesday, topping Ward Melville in extra innings. I wanted to go to that game and support my cousins and the team. But ground zero wasn't where I thought I should be. Dr. Steward agreed. So I went to extra homework help that afternoon.

Tomorrow morning, they would leave for Cooperstown and play Trommald at the historic Doubleday Field in a semi-final game. If they won, they'd play the winner of Greenvale versus Tannersville on Sunday for the Class AA State Championship. Aunt Sue and Uncle John told me they'd be driving up. Aunt Sue invited me to tag along, but I passed. I wasn't ready for anything like that. In a crazy way, I was looking forward to having the house to myself for the weekend. I needed to get used to being alone.

Aunt Sue lowered the heat on the stove. "Hi, Andy," she said.

I took a whiff of meat sauce aroma. "Hey. How's it going?"

"Good, sweetie."

"What's up with Buster? He's slacking on his greetings?"

"Oh, he's staying at our dog sitter's house for the weekend."

I looked at her quickly. "I could've watched him."

"I know, sweetheart. She has two Cavaliers. It's a little vacation for him, too."

"Ahh."

She wiped her hands with a dishtowel. "How'd school go?"

"It went. Finished up my final extra-help class with Mr. Rice."

"Good, sweetie. Any Regent exams next week?"

"Yeah. Earth Science on Tuesday."

"I'll be rooting for you." A long pause, then the question I'd known was coming: "Have you given any thought to what you want to do after you finish up school?"

I pursed my lips for a moment. "Don't know. Maybe just stay unemployed and lounge around here for a few years."

The smile on her face died.

I raised my eyebrows, pointed a finger at her. "Gotcha."

She laughed. "You think you're funny, eh?"

"Funny looking. Seriously? I have no idea what I'm going to do. Lisa works part-time as a counselor at a group home for the mentally ill. Claims she can get me on full-time there."

"Is that something you'd want to do?"

"I *do* like helping people. But … I don't know. Maybe. I figure I can try it out. And if I like it, maybe I can enroll at Suffolk Community for the spring semester. Take up psychology or something."

"That sounds like an excellent plan."

"Yeah." I pointed to the guestroom. "Gonna hit the books."

"Okay. I'll let you know when it's time to eat."

"Dinner, Andy!"

I flipped through highlighted pages in my textbook, not really seeing them, until Uncle John's voice boomed through the closed door. I popped the cap back on my highlighter. "Be right there."

I joined the family in the dining room. At the kitchen counter, Aunt Sue filled plates with spaghetti and meat sauce.

"You guys ready for your big weekend?" I gave Nathan, across the table, a smirk and pulled out a chair at what had become my spot.

Craig placed a napkin on his lap. "You know it. We're coming home with a big-ass first place trophy."

"Watch your mouth," Aunt Sue said.

"Sorry, Mom."

"Is Coach throwing you first game?" I asked.

Craig received a full plate from his mother. "Jerome's pitching tomorrow. They're saving me for Sunday."

They'd be saving Daniel for Sunday. If life was fair.

"What if you lose Saturday?" I asked.

He snorted. "We won't. But if we did, we're done. Either way, we're staying through the weekend."

"Doubleday Field is a sweet stadium," I said. "I Googled it the other day. It's like a mini pro field."

"Field has a lot of history," Nathan said around a bite of spaghetti.

"Ever been to Cooperstown, Andy?" Uncle John asked, setting his glass down.

"I think my dad took us when we were kids. Don't remember much about it, though."

"It's a neat place," he said. "I've taken these guys a few times. Been there a dozen times myself."

Aunt Sue set a plate in front of me. Sauce bubbled, a mist

of steam stretching to my face. I asked, "What time you guys heading up there?"

"Early," Nathan said. "Bus leaves from the high school at 6:00 a.m."

I opened my mouth, thinking. Beside me, Aunt Sue took her seat and reached for the parmesan cheese. "You have our cell numbers, Andy. Call us if you need anything. The fridge is stocked. Just lock up if you're going to head out."

The moment passed, I mumbled, "Okay. Will do."

I woke up quickly. The back of my head lay flat on my pillow. My breaths burst in and out. I'd been dreaming of Daniel, him pitching to me at a park in our old neighborhood. Just the two of us. It seemed so real. So damn real.

Chatter echoed through the walls. "Can you pipe down?" Uncle John called out. "Andy's sleeping."

I yawned, climbed out of bed. Pulled on tube socks and sweats then walked out to the foyer. Suitcases lined the wall beside the door.

Aunt Sue descended steps, her hair down and untamed. "Hey, Andy. It's early, why are you up?"

"Just wanna wish the guys good luck."

"Aww. Sweet."

I endured her hug then followed her into the living room. Uncle John, Craig, and Nathan sat on the couch. *Sports Center* played on the TV.

Craig stood up, a white headband squeezing his skull, dark sunglasses clipped on his collar. "What up, man?"

I focused tired eyes on him. "Not too much. Good luck. I hope you guys win it all. Make Daniel proud."

"You got it, Cuz," Craig said. "We'll win it for you, too. Both of your names are going on the plaque."

Uncle John checked his watch. "Let's get a move on, guys. We're behind schedule."

Aunt Sue came over and hugged me again. "Take care, Andy. Call us for any reason."

"You got it."

Nathan scratched at a huge pimple on his neck. "I tagged you on Facebook. Just something I made the other day. Check it out when you get a chance."

"Yeah, okay."

I stood by the window and watched Uncle John back his Hummer out of the driveway. The family was officially en route.

Free at last.

I grabbed my laptop from my bedroom, returned to the living room and logged onto Facebook. I hadn't checked my page in a while. Fake-ass people posting bold-ass lies about how great and happy their lives are. Please. I tried to stay away.

I went straight to my profile page. Nathan tagged me in a video. I clicked play.

A tribute to Daniel Lembo. A montage of photos and home-movie clips played to the background music of a gut-wrenching song.

Tears spilled down my ruined face. I could hardly catch my breath.

When it finished, I scrubbed my eyes, then I watched it again, this time pausing it on a photo of a pint-size Daniel. He was standing in front of the refrigerator at our old house, holding up a batting glove still in its plastic box. A bright smile lighting up his fleshy face. The Big B, kneeling next to Daniel, held up eight of his fingers.

What a great photo. I'd never seen it before.

I saved the photo to my desktop and clicked it open, zoomed in on the drawing that hung on the refrigerator. Daniel's art on construction paper. A stick-figure drawing of Daniel pitching to me. The scribbled title read PLAY BALL. The paper was held in place by a magnet. The magnet read COOPERSTOWN, NY.

A shiver rattled the walls of my chest.

I read it again.

Holy shit.

It couldn't possibly be a coincidence.

Breathing heavy, I kept staring at the drawing. Daniel was catching me. He was giving me the go sign.

Oh, my God. I'm going to play ball.

I snapped the laptop shut and raced into my bedroom. I didn't fully understand what was happening. But I knew I was going to make that bus.

I hurled items into an open suitcase.

Shit, my baseball stuff's still at Dad's.

Packed bags in hand, I hurried out the door. The floodlight came on, carving my path across the lawn. I pulled open the back door and hurled the bags in, launched into the driver's seat and twisted my key into the lock.

Click. Sputter.

Damn. C'mon.

I twisted the key again. More sputtering.

I sledgehammered the side of my fist against the steering wheel. "Please, God. Not now."

I turned the key again. The clunky engine turned over.

Whew. Let's go.

I drove down the block, turned into my driveway. My headlights beamed on Dad's car. I got out, leaving the heap of crap running, not wanting to risk a failed restart.

I hustled to the front door and unlocked it. Dad's snore echoed through his bedroom door.

Breathing slow, steady breaths, I tiptoed over and eased my bedroom door open. The room gleamed. Spotless. A new rug brightened the floor. Dad got rid of all Daniel's stuff. He organized *my* stuff. What the hell got into him?

I filled my bat bag with my baseball gear from the closet. Then I motored out of my house like it was on fire.

I hopped into my car and shifted into drive. The RPM kicked up, revving. A loud clanking came from the engine.

Oh, Jesus. What now?

The check engine light glowed.

I pressed my foot down on the gas. The RPM jumped, maxing … falling. Maxing … falling. I eased off the gas. It didn't help. The car shook like I was driving on railroad tracks.

I firmed up my grip on the steering wheel, my hands going numb from the vibrations, the veins on my forearms swelling. Moving forward was all that mattered. Getting to the bus. There was no way this car would make it upstate.

It just had to make it to the school.

I glanced over at the passenger seat: it was 6:06 by my cell phone. *Shit. I'm not going to make it. C'mon car, stay with me.*

I survived side roads then tested my luck on Route 25, puttering along at half the speed limit, other cars honking behind me. The school loomed in the distance.

Please let the bus still be there. Please, God.

My car squealed to a stop at a traffic light. A Greyhound bus with tinted windows stood in the lot. A row of running cars parked behind it, including Uncle John's Hummer.

Yes. Yes. C'mon, light. Let's go.

The stoplight turned green. I hit the gas. The engine revved then kicked into gear, snapping my head back. The engine knocks intensified as I steered into the parking lot. I found a spot, killed the engine. Maybe for the last time.

I'd worry about that later. Bags thumping against my legs, I ran toward the bus.

Aunt Sue, gazing out the Hummer's passenger-side window, gave me the strangest look. I kept running.

The driver, standing outside next to Coach, closed the luggage door on the lower side of the bus.

Coach followed the bus driver's gaze to me.

Breathing heavy, I said, "Got room for one more?"

Coach pulled down on the brim of his hat. His gray eyes went narrow. "Andy?"

"Coach."

"What are you doing here?"

"I'd like to come."

"To play or watch?"

"I've got my uniform."

He nodded. "You up for this?"

"I am."

He looked at the bus driver. "Have you got room for this young man's bags?"

"Of course," he said.

Standing tall, I nodded at Coach. Coach pointed at the bus door. "Let's go. You're late."

I smiled. "Yes, sir."

I climbed the bus steps, my hands shaking, my heart squeezing up my throat. I walked down the narrow aisle, my eyes on the rubbery floor. Three seats down, I stopped and looked over at Nathan.

Nathan looked out the window, his head bobbing to whatever music was playing on his iPod.

I leaned over, tapped his shoulder.

He turned and saw me. He yanked the earphones out. His jaw hung loose.

"Seat taken?" I asked.

"Andy. What the heck are you doing here?"

I sat and shushed him. "What does it look like? I'm gonna play ball, dude. Gonna help win Daniel that championship."

Nathan's lips curled up at the corners. "Really?"

"That's right."

"Nice. Cool beans."

Craig, Pete, and some of the other guys came over. Asked what I was up to. Greeted me. Welcomed me back. Not Joey. Not that I expected him to.

Coach and the bus driver boarded.

Coach walked over to me, dropped his hand on my shoulder. "Everyone, listen up. Andy Lembo has decided to come back on the team. He's here to help us win a state championship."

Hoots and roots rang out. Craig's voice echoed above the rest. "Yeah, Andy! That's my boy!"

Coach motioned his hands downward, cuing them to shut up. "Now, what do you say we go take care of business and win it all?"

More noise. Louder this time.

"All right. Settle down, guys. It'll be a long ride. Save your energy for the game."

He took a seat in the first row.

I clicked on an overhead light and closed the air vent.

Nathan elbowed me. "So, why'd you change your mind? You seemed so determined never to play again."

"I don't know. It just kinda hit me. Like this is something I should be doing."

"Well, I'm stoked you're back on the team. We're definitely going to benefit, you being back behind the plate."

A part of me wanted to tell him about the photo. About how I sensed Daniel was communicating to me from above. But just as strongly, I felt it was something special between Daniel and me. Besides, I didn't want Nathan thinking I was any more wacko than he probably already thought. I let the topic die.

Nathan dozed off by the time we merged onto the Long Island Expressway. Judging by the silence on the bus, it seemed most others had as well. I wanted to close my heavy eyes and sleep. But I kept my overhead light on, pulled out my Earth Science textbook and got to work. Not graduating this year was not an option. Plain and simple.

The sun up and bright, shadows stretched from small-town homes and stores as the bus cruised past a green-and-white sign that read "Village of Cooperstown." Trying not to think about my intensifying nausea, I sipped a ginger ale I'd picked up at the Denny's we stopped at about an hour earlier.

"Yo, there's the Hall," Pete said from the opposite side of the bus.

By the time I looked over, we had passed the Baseball Hall of Fame.

The bus arrived at our motel a little before 1 p.m. Four hours to game time.

A strong sun beat down on the parking lot while the bus driver handed out luggage, then we went into the cool of the main lobby. Players lined up, some flanked by their parents, and waited to check in.

Feeling downright ill, I browsed a rack of brochures for local attractions. Damn, I was going to have to ask my aunt and uncle if they could get me a room. Awkward. *This is why you don't decide things at the last second, Andy.*

Aunt Sue and Uncle John approached. "Andy, your jersey's in here," Aunt Sue said. "I was able to sew on the patch on the way here."

"Thanks," I said, grabbed the plastic bag from her. I'd given her my jersey at the rest area we stopped at. When I got up the nerve to mention what I wanted—to have the team patch on it—she insisted on doing it. The number 39 on a black background. Daniel's number. Now emblazoned on my jersey. I hoped I could live up to it today.

Uncle John pulled out his wallet and handed me his credit card. "You're going to need a room. Go book one."

"You sure?"

His smile was almost wider than his face. "Definitely."

I grinned. "Thanks."

Coach whistled. "Listen up, everybody."

All eyes in the lobby turned to him.

"Get settled in your rooms. Players, get dressed in your game gear. I want everyone back in the lobby no later than two o'clock. I mean it. Two o'clock. Not a second later. We're not holding the bus up for you."

After I finished at the front desk, I took the elevator up four floors and found my room at the end of the hall. I slid the card into the slot and pulled down on the silver door handle.

Sweet. I oohed and ahhed over the mediocre amenities, got comfortable on the queen-size bed and clicked on the tube. The news came on. It wasn't enough to distract me from the impending tsunami in my stomach.

As the minutes ticked away, my stomach churned more and more. I lifted up my T-shirt and watched my belly beat like a heart. My lips quivered.

Damn. I raced to the bathroom. Down on my knees, I made friends with the bowl.

After, my shaky hands gripped the counter. I stared hard at

my reflection in the mirror and said, "Is that all you've got, God? You're gonna have to do better than that. You're gonna have to kill me to keep me off the field."

I stripped down to my underwear and walked barefoot onto the room's rug and over to my bags.

Never thought I'd be putting this uniform back on. Never.

I got dressed then returned to the bathroom. I put my cap on then turned my shoulder so I could see the patch in the mirror.

We can do this, bro. Me and you. Let's go.

CHAPTER 20

THE BUS CAME TO A STOP IN FRONT OF DOUBLEDAY FIELD. I leaned forward in my seat, my clammy hands scrubbing the sides of my baseball pants.

After gathering my stuff from the overhead rack, I followed the other players off the bus. A golden sun sprayed afternoon light. I gazed at the brick stadium, its arching entranceway. The realization that I was here, really here, swept over me. But in a good way.

"Place is sick," Craig said, eyes wide.

Pete tapped my knee with the front of his bat bag. "The annual Hall of Fame game's played here. Tony Gwynn, Joe DiMaggio, Willie Mays, Ted Williams, Mickey Mantle. You name 'em. They played right where we're going to play."

I lifted my cap and brushed aside my bangs. "It's wild," I muttered.

Striding toward the stadium entrance, I squinted at a statue of a barefoot boy wearing a broad-brimmed hat, with a bat slung casually over his shoulder. Engraved on a small bronze plaque under it: The Sandlot Kid. My thoughts spun to playing ball with Daniel. To when Daniel and I played on the same travel team. Back when Dad was our coach. *Better days, for sure.* That was all I allowed myself to think about that. Safer that way.

Coach rounded up the troops and led the way into the stadium. I gazed out at the flawless baseball diamond, my heart pounding.

A gray-haired and mustached usher swung open a gate leading to the area behind home plate. He waved us in.

Fidgety, I followed the queue of players stepping through the gate. The Trommald Knights, out taking fielding practice, looked like a solid bunch, their plays crisp and smooth.

Mature trees and well-maintained homes surrounded the field. A church steeple towered above the rooftops a couple hundred yards back. An electronic scoreboard winked from behind the left field fence.

Walking in foul territory on the first-base side of the field, I turned to the empty bleachers that extended around the stadium, thirty or so rows deep. They wouldn't be empty for long.

I was sure Aunt Sue called Dad to let him know I'd be playing today. You'd think he would call and wish me good luck. Or, better yet, take the trip up and watch me play in the biggest game of my life. I didn't expect that to happen. Dad wasn't much of a baseball fan anymore. He was even less a fan of me. Still, a part of me held out hope Dad would show his face. Baseball was as close to a neutral zone as it got for us. There were times growing up when we couldn't communicate about much of anything, but we could always talk about baseball. If that was gone, all was lost.

I entered our dugout in awe. It was the first pro-style, semi-underground dugout I'd ever been in.

"Let's go, boys," Craig said, clapping quick and hard. "Let's do this."

I took a seat on the long wooden bench, reached down into my bat bag, and pulled out my cleats. Butterflies swirled in my stomach. Tension gripped my neck and shoulders.

The Knights jogged off the field.

From the dugout, Coach gazed out at the field. "Let's go, Panthers. Get loose. Then let's take fielding practice."

My legs shaky, I grabbed my fielder's mitt from the bench.

Matt Turrow, lanky and baby-faced, sat down next to me. He adjusted his baseball socks. I couldn't imagine how stressful it was for him to come up from JV and step into the starting during a playoff run. I reached my hand over to him. "Andy Lembo."

"Matt," he said, giving me a firm handshake. "Sorry about your brother."

"Thanks, man."

An eerie silence lingered, but probably only on my side. At the funeral, Coach gave me his word that I'd have my starting position back if I returned. But that was over a month ago. So who knows? I was here to play. That I knew.

Nathan walked over, slapped my shoulder with his mitt. "You wanna throw?"

I shoved my glove onto my hand. "Sure."

He grabbed a baseball from a dirt-encrusted white bucket and fled to the field.

After gathering my stuff, I followed him out.

Joey walked alongside me, his face a mess of acne, his biceps testing the elasticity of his shirtsleeves. "What up?"

"Hey, what's up?"

"You've got bigger balls than I thought. Didn't think you had it in you to come back."

Not sure of what to say, I bent my hat brim.

In a milder tone, he said, "Your brother was a good guy. Funny as hell. I really miss that kid."

We stopped on the infield dirt and turned toward each other. "Yeah, me too."

He spat on the ground. "You shouldn't have come back though."

A shiver ran through me. "Why's that?"

"Dude, your brother died on the field," he said, pointing at the mound. "On a pitch you called."

I shook my head, my teeth ground, my hands squeezed into tight fists. "What the hell's your problem?"

"I'm the only one brave enough to tell you. You're a huge distraction now. With your background, who even knows if you're stable? Nobody wants you here. Trust me."

I got up in his face and jabbed my finger at his chest. "You don't want to test a crazy person. Maybe a few weeks ago. Not now. *Trust me.*"

He shoved my hand away.

I stared him down. "You don't get it. Come tomorrow, I'll have nothing left to lose. Nothing. Insult me just once more and I swear on Daniel's grave, I will make sure you lose big time, too. I'll go to Coach and let him in on your secret. I could give two shits about what you'd do to me anymore. I'm looking forward to a good war. Go ahead. Say it again. *Test me.*"

Joey went to speak, but nothing came out. His trap slowly shut. He turned away.

"That's what I thought. Do yourself a favor and get off the stuff. It's cheating. It'll end up killing you." I punched my fist into my glove. "And, oh yeah, leave me the hell alone."

"Whatever," Joey said. He jogged off.

I meant every word. I was done being scared of Joey. I was quite sure he was done with me. That I wasn't worth his future. In a few days, school would be over. We'd go our separate ways in life. And that would be that. *Good riddance, asshole.*

I jogged out to Nathan in the outfield, my cleats clawing the green grass that had been mown in a fancy pattern.

Nathan threw me the ball, a soft toss. I caught it in my Mizuno glove, two hands. I gripped the ball and twisted it in my palm. Felt its stitches against my finger pads. *I'm back. I'm really back. This is no dream.*

I snapped the ball back to him. In my mind, though, I threw it to Daniel. I imagined Nathan's throw coming back with more zip. Imagined my palm stinging. If only I could have a catch with Daniel again. Just one more time.

After we completed fielding practice, Coach called us over. "Take a knee," he said, setting his fungo bat down on the fringe of the infield grass.

We knelt.

"I've coached a lot of teams, in many different sports. I'm most proud of this team. All teams face adversity. But not many have to deal with the death of a teammate. Daniel was family to all of us. To some of you, he was blood. It's no small feat to carry on and play hard like we have. With love and passion. Just like Daniel played it. Everyone counted us out. Now we're fourteen innings from a state championship. It's no time to let up. Play with everything you have. The time is now. Right now. Let's go, Panthers."

Adrenaline shot though my veins.

Coach picked up his clipboard from the grass. "Here's the lineup."

I sucked in a breath, held it.

"Pete Pixcell will lead us off. Left field."

I deflated, my heart still hammering.

Coach continued. "Mike Kane, shortstop. Jake Murphy, first base. Tommy Goodwin, third base. Craig Huckabee, center field. Jerome Baker, pitcher. Kevin Cross, second base. Matt Turrow, catcher. And Paul Winsor, right field."

I turned my eyes down, slumped my shoulders. How could Coach go back on his word?

Coach extended his closed fist. "All hands in."

We piled hands, did our chant. Mine came without much oomph.

Seated on the bench with the scorebook on his lap, Nathan slapped the back of his hand on my thigh. "You should be in there. It's not right."

I sat up straight, my palms pressed flat on the bench, watching Jerome Baker fire warm-up pitches to Matt. "I haven't practiced in over a month. It is what it is."

"You're better than Turrow. It doesn't make sense."

Coach entered the dugout, paying no mind to any of the benchwarmers. He sat on the other end of the bench, next to Joey, and paged through his clipboard.

Maybe Coach didn't think I was mentally ready. Maybe he was right. Heck, I was shaking, just watching them from the bench.

Why am I here, bro? There has to be a reason other than riding the pine. There has to be.

I stood up and clapped. *I'm here to make a difference. I can be the best goddamn benchwarmer.* Cupping my hands around my mouth, I yelled, "Let's go, Jerome. Here we go, Jerome. Let me hear you, infield!"

Jerome looked sharp versus the first two hitters he faced, getting both to chase bad pitches and ground out.

Their three-hole batter, laid into Jerome's first pitch, a loud ping emanating from his bat. The ball rocketed into the left-field gap and the batter coasted to second base and held up there.

That started the hit parade. Three Knights crossed home plate before all was said and done in their half of the first inning.

Jerome stormed into the dugout, his wide nostrils flaring. He flung his mitt into the brick wall behind our bench. "Relax," Coach said, glancing into the dugout on his way to the third-base coach's box. "We'll get 'em back."

Jerome rammed his backside down on the bench, massaged his forehead with his fingertips.

I got up, walked over, and sat next to him. "You okay, big guy?"

He ripped his hat off, scratched at his bald black head. "I put us in a big hole. Shit."

"Shake it off. Play your game. You're pitching way too angry out there. It's affecting your control. Take deep breaths. Focus on your rhythm, location, and mixing up pitches. You'll do fine."

He blew out breath, clapped my knee. "I know. I gotta chill. Thanks, man."

I grinned. "We'll get those runs back."

My teammates stood and cheered on Pete. I got up and joined them. Clasping the metal bar at the front of the dugout, I called out, "Let's go, Pete. Here we go, Pete!"

Their pitcher, tall and wiry, threw hard. Real hard. He sat Pete down on four pitches, nothing but gas. He had no trouble with Mike and Jake as well.

The innings cranked on. Second. Third. Fourth. Fifth. No score change. Then Trommald added a run in the sixth. They threatened more, but our infield turned a nifty double play to stop the bleeding. Our sticks stayed silent, racking a paltry four hits and plating none.

Coach yanked Jerome off the field with one down in the top of the seventh. Scott Bruno, in relief, retired the two batters he faced.

I gazed out at goose eggs marking the bottom row of the scoreboard. Three outs to go. The final inning of baseball careers looming for some. Definitely for me.

Four runs is a lot to come back on versus any team. But versus Trommald, a team with lights-out pitching and stellar defensive play, it would take a downright miracle for us.

My teammates occupied the bench, heads hanging low, faces long. Hope slipped away.

None of this made sense. I come back on the team and we lose. What kind of jinx was I?

Nathan stood up, the scorebook open in his hands. "Last licks, guys. Mike leads us off. Then Tommy and Craig. Let's go, everybody up. Finish strong."

I clapped. "Let's go. We're still in this. Big rally coming up here!"

One by one, rears rose off the pine.

Mike took good hacks, fouling off a series of pitches. Then he waved his bat on an outside fastball, hitting a high-chopper. The third baseman charged in, scooped up the baseball, and off balance, whipped the ball to first base.

One down.

I swallowed past a lump in my throat, my gaze sweeping across the field. I took it all in. The sights. The sounds. The smells. I tipped my cap. My final goodbye to the game.

"Let's do this," Nathan said.

"Yeah, let's go, Jake," I yelled, clapping hard. "Launch a moonshot, Jake. Let's go, Jake."

Jake swung through the first two pitches. Then he slapped a fly ball to left field. The left fielder trotted over and caught it.

Two down.

I paced the dugout, hardly able to watch.

Tommy lumbered toward the plate, his demeanor serious, a stark departure from his usual clownish self.

After watching the first pitch go by, Tommy poked the second pitch into right field. A base hit.

"All right," I said, clenching my fists. "We're still in this. Let's go, Craig. Keep it going."

Craig settled into the batter's box, wielding his bat like a sword.

With the count 2 and 0, the pitch rode in on Craig's thigh and he took one for the team. He didn't even try to get out of the way.

Craig shook out his leg like a dog and jogged to first.

"Let's go. Everyone up," Nathan said. "Two-out rally."

"We're in this," I said. "Let's go, Jerome. You're big here."

Like a bull, Jerome scraped his right cleat through the dirt. His chin pressed to his shoulder, Jerome waved his bat.

On a 2-1 count, Jerome chipped a low pitch into right-center field.

C'mon, drop. Drop.

The right fielder charged in, slid feet first, but couldn't reel it in. The ball bounced by him and rolled all of the way to the warning track.

"Yeah, baby. Go!" I yelled.

The center fielder raced over, grabbed the ball, spun, and flung it in to the cutoff man.

Tommy chugged as fast as his thick frame would allow and scored. Craig followed right behind him: 4-2.

Jerome hustled into third. A stand-up triple.

Kevin, the tying run, crowded the plate. Matt took practice cuts in the on-deck circle.

I wiped sweaty palms on my pants. My body buzzed with excitement. Excitement. A feeling I didn't think baseball could ever make me feel again. "Let's go, guys." I shifted my weight from foot to foot. "Do it for Daniel."

Kevin fouled the first pitch straight back into the netting.

The next pitch was high heat. Kevin swung hard and came up empty. We were down to our final strike.

God, no. Please.

Kevin readied himself, his bat held high and motionless.

The pitcher wound up, sprung forward, and spun a curve.

Kevin stayed back, waited on it, and sliced the ball down the right-field line.

Stay fair. Stay fair.

The ball splashed down on the line, kicking up white chalk. Fair ball.

"Holy crap," I screamed, pumping my fist. "Yes! Go!"

Jerome scored. Kevin hustled to second base: 4-3.

"*Woot!* Yeah, Panthers," Craig screamed.

As Jerome made his way into the dugout, my teammates and I swarmed toward him. Chanted his name. Slapped his head. Body-bumped him.

"Yeah, that's what I'm talkin' about!" Jerome hollered. "Let's go!"

Matt, representing the winning run, took slow steps toward the plate. He looked like a deer in headlights, his eyes large and round. He'd been hitless all game. Two backward Ks. You'd think Coach would give me a shot. Not that I'd want to be him in this situation. But still.

The pitcher took a deep breath, his glove steady in front of him.

My heart jackhammered.

Here we go.

The pitcher wound up, twirling his leg up like a dancer. He fired an inside fastball. Matt, jammed, swung tight and powerless. The ball dinked off his bat and rolled to the charging third baseman.

That's all she wrote.

He ate it up, fired a low throw, in the dirt to first.

The first baseman, a lefty, went to pick it, but caught only air. The ball skipped by him.

"Whoa! Holy crap. Do you believe this?" I screamed through the deafening crowd noise. Jumping, I said, "Go! Go! Go!"

The ball caromed off the wall and headed into the outfield. The right fielder juggled the ball. After grabbing hold, he fired it to the cutoff man.

Kevin cut the angle on the third base bag and scored. All tied up. Unbelievable!

Matt stood on the second base bag, hands on his knees, sucking wind.

I pushed my way through my teammates to give Kevin a high five.

Coach marched toward the dugout, his eyes hot on me. "Lembo. You're pinch running for Turrow."

Aftershocks rippled in my throat. "Okay."

Craig latched his meat hooks onto my shoulder blades. "This is your time, kid."

I nodded. A thousand thoughts sped through my mind. I selected a helmet and popped it on.

The Knights made a pitching change, and the Trommald fans cheered their hurler as he walked off the field.

I blew out a long breath and climbed the dugout steps. A sea of fans. Hundreds of eyes on me. On my scar. Oh God, what did I get myself into? *Deny the panic attack, Andy. Stay focused on the game.*

The reliever was Trommald's ace, the pitcher they were supposed to be saving for tomorrow. His expression didn't show it, but there was no tomorrow if they didn't win today.

"Way to go," I said, clapping hands with Matt as we exchanged spots.

"Win it for us," Matt said, his dimples pressed in. "Win it."

With my foot on the second-base bag, I moved my eyes over the crowd. Aunt Sue and Uncle John. No Dad. His loss.

The pitcher got loose, hurling flames to the catcher.

I thought about the game situation. Two outs. Run on anything. Take a conservative lead and don't get picked off.

Coach flashed me dummy signs.

"Batter up," the ump called out.

Paul poked the top of his bat on home plate. He'd been the King of Whiffs today, not able to catch up to the starter's heat. The reliever was throwing even harder.

Working out of the stretch, the pitcher glared at me, then back at his catcher.

I took a short lead, my shaky knees bent and my fingers wiggling at my sides. Adrenaline drenched my heart.

I watched the pitcher bring the ball and glove together. Then he kicked his leg up, and zipped a fastball in the dirt. The catcher, lunging, blocked it with his shin guard. The ball scooted away.

Instinctively, I broke for third, my head down, my legs pushing hard.

I dove headfirst, dirt clouding around me.

No throw.

My hands locked on the sides of the bag, I spat dirt.

Shit, that was dumb, Andy. You don't make the third out at third. Never.

I got up, brushed myself off.

"Way to hustle, Andy," Coach said. "There's two down. Go on the crack of the bat."

The stadium rocked, a large portion of the crowd on its feet.

Standing tall atop the third base bag, I gazed at home plate. Ninety feet away from winning this.

Clapping, I said, "Let's go, Paul. Pick one out."

I turned my shoulder inward, looked down at the black patch. Number 39.

We got this, bro. Me and you. Let's go.

I established my lead, my heart beating wildly.

The pitcher wound, snarled, and threw smoke. Paul swung a day late: 1 and 1.

Paul was overpowered on the next pitch, which blazed over the black of the plate: 1 and 2.

I danced off the bag, my fingers wiggling between my knees.

The pitcher eyed me, his mitt and ball close to his chest. He rocked into motion.

I extended my lead, skipping to my right.

The pitcher hurled a fastball in the dirt. The catcher twisted his glove, tried to backhand the ball. But it bounced off the heel of his mitt and away.

My mind clicked to the teary-eyed boy down on the train tracks. I broke for home plate. My cheeks flapped against my clenched teeth, the ground whooshed under me. My arms pumped, thighs burned.

The catcher ran for the ball, his equipment clanking. Off balance, he grabbed the ball and flicked it to the pitcher charging to home plate.

Steps before the bag, I closed my eyes and took flight. My hands and chest thumped down as the tag nailed my helmet.

My eyes still closed, I felt home plate slide under my forearms and chest.

The crowd roared.

My belly flat on dirt, I tilted my head and looked over at the ump.

The ump's arms swept through the air, he called, "Safe!"

I squeezed my eyes closed. There was Daniel, down on his knees on the train platform, giving me thumbs-up.

Holy shit. We did it. We did it.

My teammates stormed out of the dugout and piled on me. Their combined weight made it real, told me I wasn't dreaming.

Next realization: *Holy crap, we're going to play for the state championship.*

Players unstacked. Broadcasting a grin that Daniel could probably have seen from wherever he was, I popped to my feet, exchanged fives and body bumps with them.

Scanning the mess of players, coaches, and parents now on the field, I felt my smile slowly die on my face. Something inside me burned for Daniel to be among those celebrating. Heck, I'd have even settled for Dad.

While Craig and Nathan exchanged a double high five, I wanted nothing more than for Daniel and me to do our special handshake. But it wasn't going to happen. Not now. Not ever again.

Through water-glazed eyes, I pointed to the perfect sky. *One more game. For you, bro.*

CHAPTER 21

I GAZED OUT OF THE BUS WINDOW AT THE CARS PARKED IN the Best Western lot. The bus rocked to a stop. Coach stood tall in the aisle and motioned for everyone to sit. "I'm damn proud of all of you," he said. "You dug deep and came up with gold."

Hoots and hollers rang out.

"We ain't done yet. Not by a long shot."

More noise.

Coach folded his thick arms. "Okay, okay. Settle down. Go to your rooms, get changed, relax for a bit. Let's meet back up in the main lobby at 7:30 for dinner. Bring your uniforms back with you. Mrs. Bruno volunteered to do a laundry run tonight. You can pick your uniforms up at the front desk in the morning. You'll want to look sharp for our state championship game team photo."

Craig clapped loudly. "Yeah! Let's bring home a championship tomorrow, boys!"

Cheers echoed throughout the bus.

Coach smiled. "Sounds like a plan. So, main lobby at 7:30, then we'll walk to the Pizza Hut down the block. My treat. Your parents are welcome to join us. We'll have plenty of time to experience this great town tomorrow after the game. In other words, make it an early night."

A few grumbles and boos, and he said, "Seriously. Game starts at one o'clock. I want to be on the field no later than ten. Get your rest." He tipped his hat's brim. "Great job today. All of you."

Pete, sitting across from me, stuck two fingers in his mouth and whistled. I stood and brushed crusted dirt off my jersey.

Coach pointed at me. "Let's talk a minute, Andy."

I swallowed hard. "Sure thing."

He gave me a strong nod and walked away. I grabbed my bat bag and filed off the bus with the others.

My teammates headed into the hotel. I hung back, pacing small circles beyond the bus's shadow.

Coach exited the bus, an overstuffed duffel bag banging against his leg. He approached me, his lips tight and straight-lined.

"What's up, Coach?"

He scratched at the gray stubble rising from his square jaw. "I owe you an apology. I told you you'd have your starting job if you returned. On the ride up here, I gave a lot of thought to who I should start at catcher."

"It's all right, Coach. Really—"

He stuck his hand out like a traffic cop. "Hear me out. I chose Matt, not because he's the better player. He's not. But I knew what I was getting with him. He didn't lose his brother. You did. Witnessed it from behind the plate. When you came running up to the bus when we were about to leave this morning, I had to question if you were truly ready to return to the game. Understand?"

I gulped. "Yes."

"But then you went out there in a pivotal spot and showed more heart and guts than I could've imagined. You won the game for us."

I cracked a smile. "I just ran."

His eyebrows drew together. "Modest. Just like Daniel. Answer me one question. Will you be ready to start at catcher tomorrow? I mean *really* ready to start in the biggest of big games? It's okay if you say you're not. I'll understand."

My gaze fell to the pavement. My heart pounding, I thought of Daniel's reaction when he first saw me in the Panthers uniform. How he jogged over to me, his face glowing. How we did our handshake right then and there on the field.

I looked back at Coach's steely eyes. "I'll never be over Daniel's death. The game will never mean what it used to mean to me. But I can assure you this. Give me the green light tomorrow and I'll do everything in my power to help the team win. To help win Daniel that championship. That's all I can promise."

He nodded. "That's what I wanted to hear. Do me a favor."

"What's that?"

"Let Craig know you'll be catching him tomorrow."

I sat up in bed, my hands on my kneecaps, my bare feet rubbing one another. I wrestled my covers away and gazed down at my blotchy chest and quivering stomach. The pizza I consumed hours earlier shot up to my throat. I choked it back down.

I glanced at the alarm clock. 4:58 a.m.

My body felt weighted down, heavy. My eyes burned. Sleep wasn't going to happen. Not with the way my mind had been looping the same footage. Me as the catcher. A batter belting a comebacker. Craig bloodied, staggering, collapsing onto the mound.

I mopped my face. I wasn't ready. Not even close. Yesterday was different. I was riding the wave of emotion from Daniel's supposed message. I was on autopilot. Out of my usual worry-filled mind. Not today. The other voices were back. Louder voices. I had to tell Coach I made a mistake. He should start Turrow. I couldn't do it.

My airway narrowing, I hissed a breath out through pursed lips, hopped out of bed, itchy all over. A hot flash rose up my chest, scorching my face.

There's not enough air in here. I can't breathe. Why can't I breathe? Damn, I'm having a freaking panic attack. Somebody help me. Please.

I got down on my knees, closed my eyes, locked my hands behind my head and tapped my forehead on the carpet. Focused on each breath. My whole body felt adrift, a tiny little boat in rough waters, about to capsize any second.

I bit down on my lower lip, wanting to feel pain. No help.

Maybe it wasn't a panic attack.

I'm not breathing right. I have to get out of here. Now.

I stood up, legs wobbly. *Relax, Andy. Relax.*

Gasping, I threw on a pair of sweatpants and a Mets T-shirt and stuffed my bare feet into sneakers. I flipped open my cell phone. One text message reply from Lisa:

Way cool. good luck, sweetheart!!! Will try 2 make it up it there 2mor :)

Great, even more pressure. I grabbed my room card and wallet from the desk and out the door I went.

The knot in my stomach tightened as I made my way through the lobby and out double doors that parted at my approach. Warm, fresh air slapped my face.

Walking briskly, I cut across the Best Western parking lot and headed up the shoulder of Route 28. The occasional car passed me. A couple of them slowed. I kept marching forward, unable to outpace thoughts of a comebacker striking Craig's head.

About a mile away from the motel, a host of light poles rose from a forest of green trees. Ball field lights. A high-arching sign in the distance read, "Cooperstown Dreams Park."

I walked up to a fence at the side of the road. *I know this place,* I thought. It was a park just for Little Leaguers. Little Leaguers with well-off parents. I remembered a friend from upstate who had played there in a weeklong tournament. He played the video and boasted. I was jealous, for sure. How could I not be? A week of nothing but baseball. A whole crapload of replica-pro fields with short porches. Baseball-themed cabins to sleep in. The definition of paradise for me back then.

As jealous as I was of my friend, my insides didn't burn with envy like Daniel's. To Daniel, Disney World had nothing on Cooperstown Dreams Park. And our talentless friend got to play there. Not Daniel, the phenom.

I looked up at the intense blue sky, and could almost see Daniel rolling his eyes as I whispered my friend's name. I looked down at the dirt before my feet, at the fence surrounding the park, then back at the sky. "I hear you loud and clear, bro. He had his day. Today's our day."

I spat mouthwash into my hotel room's bathroom sink, grabbed my folded uniform off the floor, and suited up. I stared hard at my reflection in the bathroom mirror. Twisted my hat down. Squared my jersey on my shoulders.

My thoughts rolled to Dad. *What could he possibly be doing that he can't pick up the phone and wish his son good luck before the freaking state championship game? My last game.*

That was the kind of shit I'd expect from The Bitch. But Dad was a better person than Mom. Much better. Dad didn't press an iron to my face. He didn't run out on Daniel and me. He stuck by us. Raised us by himself. Sure, I downright hated him a lot of the time, but he had made time to coach Daniel and me every year. Spent his summers driving us for away games. He was there. And I thought he always would be.

Or, he had been there. Until Daniel's gift became obvious, I thought he loved me unconditionally. Guess Daniel was the only one he really loved.

I flicked off the bathroom light, then went into the bedroom and gathered my stuff. Fifteen minutes later, I joined the crowd gathered outside by the bus.

After all players were accounted for and the luggage stowed, Coach whistled. "Let's go." I followed the flow of players into the bus. Shoved my bat bag onto the overhead rack. Sat in the fourth row.

My breaths tightened. My heartbeats smacked my ribcage. A bitter pit lodged in my stomach.

Focus on baseball, Andy. Just baseball.

Quiet chatter, nervous energy from my teammates, filled the bus. I wiped my sweaty palms down my seat, questioning if I was ready. I mean *really* ready.

CHAPTER 22

NATHAN WALKED OVER, SLAPPED HIS MITT ON MY KNEE. "Wanna throw?"

It was four hours till game time and the Tannersville Tigers hadn't arrived yet. I slid my bat bag under the dugout bench and swapped sneakers for cleats.

The Tigers played a marathon of a game yesterday. Fourteen innings. Burned through their two best pitchers. A lucky break for us.

I took a deep breath and climbed the dugout steps. The sun roasted my neck. Clenching a tattered baseball in my fielder's glove, I moved my eyes over the perfect field and rows of empty bleachers.

Nathan punched his glove.

I crow-hopped, but didn't launch the ball.

Nathan's stare had drifted to the grandstand behind me. His face serious, he took off his glove.

I looked over my shoulder.

Dad. Holy shit.

I tucked the ball in my glove, an unexpected wave flooding my heart.

Dad, field level, looked out from behind the chain link fence over by the dugouts. I walked toward him, a lump expanding in my throat.

Dad looked down, his fingers fidgeting with the brim of a Mets cap. He lifted his gaze and found my eyes. Hard lines marked his tired, unshaven face.

My long shadow stretched to Dad's sneakers. I took off my glove. "Dad."

"Son." Dad gave a slight nod.

I pushed down the latch, opened the gate. He hiked up his jeans, stepped into the area behind home plate. His eyes moved over the stadium. "Some place."

"It really is."

"Heard you won the game for the team yesterday."

Yeah, where were you? "I was just a pinch runner."

He lifted his Mets hat, wiped a forearm across his sweaty forehead. "It took guts to go back to school. To come here and play again."

"Thanks." I choked the word out.

"Listen, I can't change what happened. I was drunk. I was wrong."

I gulped. "It's okay, Dad."

"No, it's not. I owe you an apology. I'm sorry, Andy. You're no loser. I'm … proud of you."

A shiver plunged down my spine. My eyes watery, I went to speak, but no words came out.

Dad cleared his throat. "I love you, son. Don't ever think I don't."

A tear trickled down my scarred cheek. I wiped my face dry with the back of my hand. "I love you, too, Dad."

"Maybe after this game is over, you and I can spend some time in this great town." His lips stretched thin.

"Sounds good."

His misty eyes went narrow. "Daniel would've loved to play here."

Goose bumps blanketed my arms. I glanced at the mound and imagined Daniel strutting toward it, a goofy smile on his glowing face. "I know he would."

"Our family will never be the same. But that doesn't mean we can't be a family. When we get back home, I'd like you to move back in with me. We can start over. A clean slate."

I sniffled. "That could work. But … I'm not Daniel. I'll never be Daniel. But Daniel never expected me to be. I'll only come back home if you stop expecting so much from me. Maybe we could go to counseling together or something."

I didn't know what was going on inside his head in that long moment, but finally, his eyes wrinkled at the corners. "Maybe we should."

I nodded. "All right then."

He stuck out his hand.

I shook it.

He pulled me into a hug. I closed my eyes, tapped my fist and glove on his back until he released me.

He blew out a long breath. "I'll let you get back. You guys have a state championship to win."

I shoved my glove on and punched the ball into it. "Thanks for coming. Means a lot."

He nodded.

Jogging back to Nathan, I looked out at the church steeple, the white clouds. All of my family who mattered was here. I could do this. I had to go the distance.

Seated on the dugout bench, I strapped on shin guards.

"Let's go, guys," Craig said, clapping his glove as he climbed out of the dugout. "Play big."

I stood up, my heart pushing its way up my throat, my breaths going shallow.

Nathan poked me with the corner of the scorebook. "Let's go, Lembo. Show 'em how it's done."

I grabbed my glove and mask off the bench. "Here goes nothing."

I walked out to the field, my eyes nervously darting side to side at the sea of fans. Way more people than I'd ever played in front of. I hoped I wouldn't make a fool of myself.

Craig worked his cleat into the dirt gracing the pitching rubber. I spotted Dad, Uncle John, Aunt Sue, and Lisa seated together in the grandstand.

Lisa waved.

I smiled and nodded.

I put on my mask and assumed a catcher's stance, hardly able to breathe.

While Craig fired warm-up pitches, thoughts of Mattelson ripping a comebacker ambushed my mind.

"Batter up," the ump called out.

I peered through the metal mask bars at the leadoff batter. A short, stocky kid, a black and orange uniform. He took big cuts in the on-deck circle.

"Let's go, George. Start us off, George," a deep voice rang out from the Tigers' dugout.

George settled into a batting stance, hips in motion. I adjusted my mask, shifted my target over to the outer half of the plate. Choked out a few breaths.

C'mon, Andy, focus.

I gave Craig the curveball sign. Craig shook it off.

Damn. I gave him the sign I knew he wanted. Fastball.

He nodded. I brought my closed fist behind my back. The ground seemed to be swaying. A seasick feeling. Silver sparks flashed in my vision.

Not a panic attack. Not now. How am I going to do this, bro? This is only the first batter!

Craig wound up, his left leg kicked high, then he exploded forward, the ball spinning off his fingertip. I flinched as the baseball drilled into my glove.

I returned the ball, thinking about vehicles, lights flashing, cruising down to the field.

Craig licked his lips, his glove held steady in front of his chest. I pictured him bloodied, dropping onto the mound. I gulped air, my heart beating wildly. Sweat moistened my face and back.

Craig stared in at me, waiting for signs. I called for a timeout, stood. Jogged out to him.

"What up, man?" he asked.

I looked down at the mound dirt. "I think I made a mistake. I don't think I can do this."

"What do you mean?"

"I'm not cut out for this. I'm going to have a panic attack on the field."

He tapped me with his glove. "Cuz. Look at me."

I did.

He wiggled the brim of his hat. "I can't tell you what to do. But know this. I want to pitch to you, not Turrow. I know you're no quitter, and if you walk off this field it's going to haunt you forever."

"I know."

He patted his hand on his heart. "Play from here. Down deep. Forget what your head's telling you. Have no fear. Play from your heart. For the love of the game. Just like Daniel did. Daniel's watching. I know he is."

The field ump walked over. "Let's go. Break it up."

I looked over at Coach pacing the dugout. Even if Joey hadn't been lying, no doubt, Coach was questioning his decision to start me.

If a panic attack happens, so be it. Bring it on. I can't let fear rule me. Not today. Not anymore. A flock of birds soared over the church steeple. I punched my fist into my palm of my mitt. "Let's whiff this kid."

Craig grinned. "That's the Andy I know."

I jogged back to my position and got down, my glove extended. My focus sharp on the game, I gave Craig an inside fastball sign.

Craig wound up and, fired heat. George chopped the ball to the shortstop. Mike swept it up and fired a bullet to first.

I lifted my mask. "Nice play, Mikey. One down."

The next two hitters singled. Runners marked the corners.

The cleanup batter looked like a goddamn lumberjack. Broad shoulders. Tree trunks for legs. I tried not to think of Mattelson. But in doing so, I did just that.

Focus on the game, Andy. The game. Love the game. No fear.

I adjusted my cup and gave Craig an outside fastball sign. Craig nodded, rocked into motion. His pitch came down Broadway.

Lenny swung hard, the ball pinging off his bat. A deep drive to left field.

Pete raced back, leaped, his arm stretched over his head. But he came up empty. Pete misplayed the ball's ricochet and the ball bounced to the wall. The batter rounded the bases with lighting speed. He blurred by me. An inside-the-park homerun: 3-0, Tigers.

Damn. But I couldn't let my team down, not now. My mask in my hand, I said, "Shake it off, Craig. Let's get the next guy."

Craig muttered to himself, his cheeks blazing.

The ump threw Craig the ball. Craig snatched it, rubbed it down, found his rhythm and closed down the first inning with a steady stream of gas.

"We'll get 'em back," I said, walking beside him back to the dugout.

"Damn, I gave that kid a meatball. Knew it once it left my hand."

"Don't sweat it. You came back strong. We're good."

Except for me. I wasn't good at all. Stomach churning, I went into the dugout, peeled off my catcher's gear. I pulled my batting glove onto my trembling left hand and patted the Velcro strap flat.

The Tigers warmed up on the field, not a weak player among them. Everything about them said "precision." Their shortstop had put on a show earlier, making the position look easy, his glove a vacuum, his arm a cannon.

I stood up from the bench and stretched out my back. Tension weighed on me.

"Start us up, Andy," Nathan said, slapping my butt.

I selected a helmet from the rack and popped it on. Then I grabbed my bat, a black Easton.

I stepped out of the dugout. Hundreds of eyes on me.

Their thick-boned southpaw got loose on the mound, his pitches packing decent zip.

I took warm-up swings in the on-deck circle, trying to time his slow, unconventional windup.

The catcher stood and threw the ball down to second base.

"Batter up," the ump called out.

I knocked the bat handle on the ground, freeing the doughnut from the barrel. My teammates cheered me on.

I walked up to the batter's box, belly juices swirling. I turned and looked at Coach. He worked his hands over his face and body. Nothing brewing.

The outfielders moved in. The crowd noise picked up. So did my heart rate.

This is it. No going back.

I stepped into the batter's box, right hand raised to signal time out, left hand clamped on the bat handle.

We can do this, bro. We are *doing this.*

The pitcher planted his cleats on the rubber. Sweat moistened his swollen face and neck. His eyes went hard and narrow. I jammed my hands together, then curled my shoulder inward and gazed at the black patch. I cocked my right elbow and waved the bat.

I got low and watched an inside fastball whiz by me. Strike one.

Damn, he was good.

I choked up on the bat and ground my teeth.

Once again, the pitcher wound up and fired flat heat.

My emotions packed, I grunted as I swung. I laid metal on the ball, belting a line drive down the left-field line.

I tossed the bat away, tore down the baseline.

The first base coach, called out, his arm whirling, "Go. Go. Take two. Take two!"

Sprinting, I glanced at the left fielder as he tracked down the skipping ball. I cut the angle on the first-base bag, put my head down and motored to second. A stand-up double.

Cheers resonated. My body buzzed. I locked my hands on my kneecaps, my left foot staked on the bag. I looked over at my teammates exchanging high fives in the dugout. Smiles on their faces.

Coach flashed me meaningless signs. I established a conservative lead, fingers wiggling at my sides.

Working out of the stretch, the pitcher regarded me out of the corner of his eye.

Pete slapped the ball to the right side of the infield. I pivoted and took off.

The grounder had eyes, finding its way between the second and first basemen. Coach waved me home. "Go, go, go!"

I rounded third then really floored it, legs and arms pumping hard. My cleat stamped home plate. *That's one run back.*

Winded, I pointed to the sky, a slight gesture but enough. *For you, bro. That one's for you.*

Teammates swarmed me. Bumped and slapped my body. Adrenaline roared through my veins. In the dugout, I yanked off my helmet and brushed back my bangs. Craig massaged my shoulders. "Way to get us going. You got wheels, kid."

I placed my helmet back on the rack.

Tommy came over, his hand held high. "Nice, Andy."

I slapped him five.

It didn't take long for the pitcher to find his groove. He got Mike to pop out then caught Jake looking on a cutter.

"Let's go," Craig said. "Two-out rally."

In the corner of the dugout, I put my gear back on.

Soon, the Tigers were jogging off the field, ahead 3-1. I pulled my mask down and headed out to the field, envisioning myself an armored warrior. Ready to battle again.

As the innings cranked on, the sun blazed hotter, but our bats went ice cold. The Tigers, playing near flawless baseball, went up 4-1 in the fourth inning and 5-1 in the fifth.

With two outs and nobody on in the top of the seventh, Craig waved me to the mound. I took off my mask, jogged out to him. "What's up?"

He rubbed down the baseball. "Just wanted to say you played a hell of a game back there. You have a lot to be proud of, Cuz. Regardless of how this thing ends."

I smiled. "We both did Daniel proud."

"No doubt, kid."

I stuck out my closed first. He knuckled into mine. I pulled my mask down. "Let's get this last guy. Then stage a great comeback. Just like yesterday."

Even though the score didn't reflect it, Craig was pitching a solid game. His baseball career had legs. He had already accepted a baseball scholarship to St. John's University. I was sure he'd do big things there.

He winked. "Let's do it."

I jogged back behind the plate and got into position, knowing this could be the final pitch I would catch in a real game. Ever.

I flashed him signs. Outside fastball. He nodded, wound up.

The batter swung, popped the ball up to left field.

Pete drifted in and squeezed it. I took off my mask, turned around and gazed at the crowd. Dad, Aunt Sue, and Uncle John were standing, clapping. I nodded, blew out a breath, and retreated to the dugout.

Nathan clapped my shoulder. "You caught a great game out there, Cuz."

I removed my armor. "Thanks," I said.

"Top of the seventh, guys," Nathan called out, looking down at the scorebook. "Last chance. Here's the order. Cross. Winsor. Then the top. We came back yesterday. Let's do it again."

Craig clapped. "Everybody up," he said. "Finish strong."

Patting a batting helmet on, I joined my teammates' cheers. "Pick one out, Kev. Drive one. Let's go, Kevin. Start us up. Everyone hits."

Kevin grounded out. One down.

I grabbed my bat and headed to the on-deck circle. "Let's go, Paul. You're big here. Start a rally."

Paul took good cuts, but he ended up popping out to the shortstop. Two down.

Please don't let me make the last out. Please.

Craig chanted my name, loud. Soon my other teammates got into the act. Even the crowd joined in. "Andy! ... Andy! ... Andy!"

A strong breeze blew out of nowhere, swept across my face.

I stepped into the batter's box, my fear and tension suddenly gone. My knees bent, my bat waving, I imagined Daniel and me as kids playing ball in our backyard back in Rochester. Just the two of us. Relaxed. Having a great time.

The pitcher wound up, fired a low pitch. Ball one.

I imagined Daniel cheering me on. "Let's go, Andy. Give the ball a ride!"

As soon as the ball came out of the pitcher's hand, I had a bead on the fastball. I swung hard, put my hips into the swing. The ball rocketed off the bat, skipped into left field.

I hustled to first base and held there. Pete pointed at me. I pointed back.

My foot on the base, I clapped and called out, "C'mon, Pete. Keep us going."

Pete settled into a batting stance. I took a healthy lead, ready to make this comeback happen.

Once more, the pitcher wound up, pitched high heat. Pete chased it, skied the ball to left field. I bolted, my head down, my arms pumping.

Throwing a glance to the outfield, I watched the leftfielder drift back and catch the final out.

We lost. It was over.

Almost.

I'm going the distance. I kept running.

I clapped Coach's hand as I rounded third base. I chugged on, running right across home plate.

The Tigers piled on one another over by the mound, every bit deserving of the championship.

I took off my batting helmet, tucked it under my arm and gazed up into the crowd.

Dad gave me a thumbs up.

Lisa lifted a cardboard sign: "#5 and #39, Battery Brothers Forever!"

Nathan jogged out to me and put his arm around my shoulders. "You played your heart out. Daniel's smiling somewhere."

A lump swelling in my throat, I said, "I know he is."

I imagined Daniel and me doing our handshake, capped with a chest bump.

Love you, bro. Always.

"Hold on. I'll walk you to your car," I said to Lisa outside the stadium.

Lisa said her goodbyes to my family. Then off we went, an awkward silence stretching between us.

Our pace slowed as we approached her car. She shook keys out of her purse and unlocked the doors. "I'm glad your dad showed."

I leaned my bat bag against the side of her car. "Yeah."

"You guys need each other."

I took off my baseball cap and ran my fingers through my sweaty hair. "Guess we'll see how it goes. We're all gonna check out the Hall of Fame in a bit. Y'sure you don't want to come?"

She reached out, touched her fingers to the back of my hand. "Wish I could, sweetheart."

My fast-beating heart pounded in my ears.

Maybe it was the caring way she said it. Or her soft touch. Or the way the sunlight brought out the sparkle in her eyes. A sparkle I hadn't noticed before.

Or maybe it was her new hairstyle, pulled up and back, showing off just how pretty her face was.

Her weight didn't seem to matter anymore. Never should have. I could almost hear Daniel asking me, just as he had before our first double date, *It's what's on the inside that counts, right, champ?*

I screwed up courage and asked, "What do you think of me?"

She bit the corner of her mouth. "That's easy. You're a great person. A great friend."

I waved off her comment. "I don't mean that. Look at my face. This scar. I mean, would you, you know, ever consider dating a guy like me?"

"No. Never."

"Oh." I showed her the top of my head. "Can't blame you."

"A guy *like* you, no. You? *Of course.*"

Breathing became difficult. "Really?"

"You're so handsome, Andy. Especially in that uniform. Any girl would be lucky to date you."

Sweat cooled on my neck. "So, maybe we could go to a movie or something some night?"

She tilted her head to the side, her eyes catching sunlight. "Like a date?"

"Not like a date. A date."

"Andy," she said, choked with emotion. "I'd love that."

Her words hammered home. My pulse fluttering, I leaned in and kissed her lips.

We smiled at each other and kissed again.

I held her hand and glanced over my shoulder at the baseball stadium. In every baseball game, on every play, there were endless possibilities. Maybe something routine would happen. Or funny. Or horrific. Or amazing.

Possibilities. Hope.

Life was no different.

Game on.